125 best
Food
Processor
recipes

George Geary

Robert
ROSE

125 Best Food Processor Recipes
Text copyright © 2005 George Geary
Photographs copyright © 2005 Robert Rose Inc.
Cover and text design copyright © 2005 Robert Rose Inc.

For complete cataloguing information, see page 182.

Disclaimer

The recipes in this book have been carefully tested by our kitchen and our tasters. To the best of our
knowledge, they are safe and nutritious for ordinary use and users. Some recipes contain raw egg yolks for
which substitutions have been supplied. For those people with food or other allergies, or who have special
food requirements or health issues, please read the suggested contents of each recipe carefully and determine
whether or not they may create a problem for you. All recipes are used at the risk of the consumer.

We cannot be responsible for any hazards, loss or damage that may occur as a result of any recipe use.

For those with special needs, allergies, requirements or health problems, in the event of any doubt,
please contact your medical adviser prior to the use of any recipe.

Design & Production: PageWave Graphics Inc.
Editor: Carol Sherman
Recipe Tester: Jennifer MacKenzie
Copy Editor: Karen Campbell-Sheviak
Photography: Mark T. Shapiro
Food Styling: Kate Bush
Prop Styling: Charlene Erricson

Cover image *(counter-clockwise from left)*: Blue Cheese Peanut Coleslaw (page 41), Roasted Red Pepper
Guacamole Dip (page 30), Citrus Bliss Cheesecake (page 151) and Roasted Pecan Pumpkin Soup (page 59)

The publisher and author wish to express their appreciation to the following supplier of props used in the
food photography:

Caban
396 St. Clair Avenue West,
Toronto, Ontario M5P 3N3
Tel: (416) 654-3316
www.caban.ca

We acknowledge the financial support of the Government of Canada through the Book Publishing Industry
Development Program (BPIDP) for our publishing activities.

Published by Robert Rose Inc.
120 Eglinton Avenue East, Suite 800, Toronto, Ontario, Canada M4P 1E2
Tel: (416) 322-6552 Fax: (416) 322-6936

Printed in Canada
1 2 3 4 5 6 7 8 9 FP 13 12 11 10 09 08 07 06 05

Miss Catherine Goeckel
1910-2005
She never stopped learning

Contents

Acknowledgments 6

Introduction 7

    Equipment and Safe Usage. 7

    Basic Processor Parts. 7

    Hand Tools and Equipment. 9

    Ingredients and How to Process Them. . . 11

    Sources 14

Appetizers. 15

Salads and Salad Dressings 35

Soups. 51

Main Courses. 63

Vegetables. 85

Yeast Breads and Rolls 99

Cookies and Brownies 117

Pies, Tarts and Pastries. 133

Cakes and Quick Breads. 149

Sauces 173

Index 183

Acknowledgments

I COULD NOT HAVE WRITTEN this remarkable book without the help of my family, friends and the many food professionals I have known over the years.

I thank my parents for purchasing my first food processor in 1979 for my birthday. Mom is my biggest supporter of my work. Thanks Dad for all the great advice, and Monica and Patti for being my two roses. Thanks Neil for being understanding of my travel and work schedule, Jonathan for keeping my office in order; and Teri Pittam for being my office assistant and primary recipe tester. Thanks Lee Wooding for taking a chance on having an unknown teacher instruct at your school and now with the staff at Cuisinart, Mary Rodgers and the entire Cuisinart Test Kitchen Staff, and Lisa Ekus, my good friend for many years who turned into my agent.

I also express my gratitude to Carol Sherman, my editor, for her guidance and many long hours on the phone and Internet in making our third book together a pleasure; Bob Dees, my publisher and friend at Robert Rose, for his great direction on my books; and, Jennifer MacKenzie, for going beyond just testing my recipes but giving them life and my voice.

And, finally, thanks to all of my many students and the cooking schools and directors throughout the country.

Introduction

THE FOOD PROCESSOR IS MAGICAL. You can create such great things with this machine. It's time saving, too. It can cut your kitchen prep time in half. Yet when I talk about food processors in my culinary classes and workshops I get a sigh. Most of the students have them but don't use them daily like I do. I wondered why. The answer was cleanup. Most recipes require you to clean the work bowl three to four times within a recipe. In this book you only have to clean the bowl at the end of the recipe. In the cookie chapter you can even start at the beginning of the chapter and make every single recipe without cleaning the bowl for the entire chapter.

Equipment and Safe Usage

When you remove your food processor from its box for the first time, it can be an enlightening and overwhelming experience — all those parts, blades and bowls. This section will help you understand how to get more use from your processor and how it works. Safety is a big issue with food processors. Years ago you could get a finger caught or food lodged in the working blades. Today most processors have stopping mechanisms and locking devises to prevent injury. Before you start to use your food processor, check your machine and read the manual and any other literature that came with it.

I teach in a different cooking school almost every night and have used a variety of food processor brands. I've gotten to know most of the makes, models and varieties available on the market today. Before adding any food to the machine, I put all of the parts together and then turn it on to make sure I'm familiar with the way it works. I call this a dry run. I even do this in front of the class. It saves time and trouble if the machine is assembled correctly before you start. It can be frustrating and messy if you have to take the machine apart with the work bowl filled with ingredients.

Basic Processor Parts

Base: This is the only part of the food processor that cannot be submerged in water. It houses the motor and cord for power. The base unit has a touch pad or buttons with On, Off and Pulse. Some more advanced machines also have a dough button, which can be used when making bread so the machine doesn't overheat.

Work Bowl: The bowl in which all of the ingredients are processed, shredded or chopped.

Cover/Feed Tube: This covers the work bowl. It usually has a large vertical feed tube area for use with vegetables and cheese. Food is pushed with the pusher through the feed tube when slicing or grating or when adding additional ingredients while the processor is running. For safety, in most of the later models you must have the complete cover, feed tube and pusher assembled for the machine's motor to run.

Pusher: The pusher is generally used with the slicing or shredding blade. The pusher guides the food through the feed tube onto the blade in the work bowl. It lifts up out of the feed tube; you place the ingredient on top of the blade and re-insert the pusher on top. The pusher then triggers an activating rod in the work bowl, which causes the motor to start.

Small Feed Tube: This fits inside the pusher. I normally keep it locked in place unless I need to incorporate something while the machine is running. Mostly only liquids, an egg or small amounts of dry ingredients can fit through this opening. The tube often has a drip hole in the bottom for dripping oils or other ingredients. It is great to use when making a mayonnaise.

Blades

Metal blade: This all-purpose blade, also known as a steel blade, is the one you'll use the most for processing and pulsing ingredients. It's also used for chopping, puréeing and blending. The blade is very sharp. Think of it as two knives side by side. When removing food from the work bowl, take the bowl off of the base of the machine, leaving the blade in place, then put your forefinger in the hole underneath and your thumb on the bottom edge of the bowl so you can hold the blade in the bowl. Tip the bowl over and dump your ingredients into the pan or bowl. Then grip the plastic blade hub and remove the blade from the bowl, carefully scraping food off with a spatula. Using

the spatula, scrape out any remaining food from the work bowl.

When processing with the metal blade you'll see the blade spinning very fast. When you turn the motor off, you want the blade to stop almost on a dime. This is a good test when you're looking to purchase a machine. When processing, the blade spins the ingredients as it cuts them.

Some recipes require you to pulse rather than process. The reason for this is that when you pulse, the blades pick up the ingredients and throw them to the sides of the bowl. The ingredients then fall back down to the bottom of the work bowl and again they are picked up and thrown to the sides. Pulsing makes the food jump.

Dough blade: Dough blades are either plastic or metal. Both work in the yeast recipes. The dough blade looks like the metal blade but is much shorter and the tips are somewhat bent down. The dough blade is not sharp and cannot cut ingredients like the metal blade. Store your blade in a protective sleeve or a see-through bag. Check your manual for the recommended minimum amount of flour to be used with the dough blade. You may need to use the regular blade for smaller recipes.

Slicing blade or disk: In some machines you have to install a separate stem to use this blade. This stem is used for all of the blades except the metal blade. The stem is attached to the bottom of the slicing blade and then placed in the base of the machine. Some machines come with a few slicing blades of different sizes. You can purchase additional blades on the manufacturer's website or at the store where you purchased your machine. Before cleaning and storing, disconnect the stem from the blade and keep separately. Store the blade in a protective sleeve or a see-through bag. Some companies make a specially designed case for blades that comes with some models or can be purchased separately.

Shredding blade or disk: Again, in most cases, you will need to assemble this blade with the stem in order to use it. It will shred all your hard and semi-hard cheeses. There are different size shredding blades available for some machines. As with the slicing blades, you can purchase additional blades on the manufacturer's website or at the store where you purchased your machine.

Hand Tools and Equipment

The first step in creating a perfect recipe every time is having the proper tools. The wrong-size pan or poor-quality tools will cause problems that are not easy to solve. Many of the tools that you'll need will have other uses in your kitchen and last a long time, so it's worth purchasing quality equipment the first time. You'll never have to replace it.

Hand Tools

Rubber spatulas
A rubber spatula is the perfect tool for scraping the work bowl clean. It also allows for the most thorough mixing of ingredients, the least waste of ingredients when turning them into the baking dish and an easy cleanup. The new silicone spatulas, which are heatproof to 1000°F (538°C) are ultra-efficient because they can go from the mixing bowl to the stovetop. Commercial-quality spatulas are more flexible and durable than grocery-store brands. Make sure that the metal blade is out of the work bowl before scraping the sides because the blade can cut into the rubber spatula.

Whisks
Whisks come in many sizes for different jobs. If you buy only one whisk, select a medium-size one. I prefer mine with a wooden handle because they last longer. In this book, I use the whisk to blend ingredients in a saucepan or in a small bowl for salad dressings and sauces.

Liquid measuring cups
The most accurate way to measure liquid ingredients is with a glass or Pyrex® measuring cup with a pouring spout. They are widely available in sizes ranging from 1 cup (250 mL) to 8 cups (2 L). Place the measure on a flat surface and add the liquid until it reaches the desired level. When checking for accuracy, bend over so that your eye is level with the measure. New models of liquid measures are now available that allow you to measure the ingredients without bending because the markings are inside the cup for easy viewing. Pyrex® cups can also be used in the microwave to melt butter and heat water.

Dry measuring cups

The most accurate way to measure dry ingredients is with metal nesting measuring cups. They usually come in sets of four to six cups in sizes ranging from ¼ cup (50 mL) to 1 cup (250 mL). Spoon the dry ingredient into the appropriate cup and then level off by sliding the flat end of a knife or spatula across the top of the cup. The exceptions are brown sugar and shortening, which need to be packed firmly in the cup for correct measurement.

Measuring spoons

The most accurate measuring spoons are metal. A set of sturdy spoons ranging from ⅛ tsp (0.5 mL) to 1 tbsp (15 mL) is necessary for measuring small amounts of both liquid and dry ingredients.

Mixing bowls

A nested set of small, medium and large mixing bowls will be used countless times. Having the right size bowl for the job, whether it's beating in egg whites or whipping a quart (1 L) of cream, helps the cooking process. Ceramic, glass and stainless steel all have their merits, but I think stainless steel is the most versatile.

Microplane® zester/grater

A Microplane® zester/grater with a handle is the best tool for quickly making zest from lemons or other citrus fruits. It is also good for grating hard cheeses and chocolate.

Offset spatula

This tool has a long handle and a flexible metal blade that is set at an angle. It's ideal for smoothing out batters in pans without dragging your knuckles through the mixture and is great for spreading icing over cakes. Offset spatulas come in a variety of lengths and thicknesses. Choose one that feels comfortable in your hand.

Baking Pans

The note to purchase once and use forever bears repeating for baking pans. Invest in quality pans; they conduct heat more efficiently, so cooking is more even and the desired results are achieved on top and bottom. Have an assortment of baking pans on hand for the most flexibility in making a variety of recipes.

A good selection of pans would include:
- 9-inch (23 cm) metal pie pan
- 9-inch (23 cm) ceramic quiche pan
- 10-inch (3 L) metal Bundt pan
- 13-by 9-by 2-inch (3 L) glass baking dish
- 17-by 11-inch (43 by 28 cm) or 15-by 10-inch (38 by 25 cm) baking pan
- Regular and mini metal muffin tins

Saucepans, skillets and stockpots

Never have there been so many choices in this area of cookware. Look for a high-quality pan. I use All-Clad Stainless in my kitchen. If a set is beyond your budget and you are not sure if you will like a certain brand, I suggest that you purchase one of the small pans first and give it a try. Then, if you're pleased go back and purchase a set. Be wary of discount stores that offer pots and pans at reduced prices: these are often seconds or special purchases that include pots with wobbly handles, off-center bottoms and other flaws.

A good selection of pots and pans for the recipes in this book would be:

- 9-inch (23 cm) skillet (nonstick or metal finish is fine)
- 10-inch (25 cm) skillet (nonstick or metal finish is fine)
- 8-qt (8 L) stockpot
- 6-qt (6 L) stockpot
- 4-qt (4 L) saucepan

Ingredients and How to Process Them

Dairy Products
Liquid milk products
I use whole milk in all of the baking recipes and 2% milk in the savory dishes. When I use cream it is whipping (35%) cream. Processing whipping cream in the work bowl with the metal blade results in a thickened cream. Some processors state that you can achieve a thick whipped cream, ready to top a pie. I have only ever been able to achieve this by using the optional beaters that you can purchase for the larger machines.

Cheeses
Cream cheese
Cream cheese is a fresh cheese made from cow's milk and by law must contain 33% milk fat and no more than 55% moisture to be classified as such.

- *Neufchâtel cheese* is a reduced-fat cream cheese that contains 23% milk fat, which means fewer calories.

- *Light or lower-fat cream cheese* has about half the calories of regular cream cheese. Whipped cream cheese, which is soft because it has air whipped into it, has slightly fewer calories. Non-fat cream cheese, of course, has no calories from fat and is best used on a bagel or sandwich, not for baking.

Use a name brand cream cheese. Some of the store brands contain added ascorbic gum acids and moisture, which diminish the texture and quality of the baked goods. To process cream cheese, cut into small pieces and place around the work bowl. Then, replace the cover and process according to the recipe.

Hard cheeses
Parmesan and **Romano** cheeses are used throughout the book. These cheeses are hard and somewhat difficult to process unless you cut into chunks and feed through the feed tube while the motor is running.

Semi-soft cheeses
Cheddar, **Swiss**, **Jack** and other similar cheeses are very easy to process. Make sure that you cut the cheese into small pieces so it fits in the feed tube for slicing or shredding.

Soft cheeses
Provolone, **mozzarella** and other soft cheeses may look like they would be simple to process with the shredding blade. However, the cheese is more likely to pack onto the blade, turning some of it into a creamy, soft substance.

Place the cheese in the freezer first for about 20 minutes prior to shredding. This hardens the cheese so it will shred more easily.

Blue cheese is aptly named because it has blue veins running through it — a result of being treated with molds and ripened. The aging process intensifies the flavor of the cheese, which is popular in salads and salad dressings and served with fruit. It is also used in cooking. The texture is firm enough for crumbling. My favorites are Porte Reyes Blue Cheese from northern California and Maytag Blue from Iowa. Well-known names for international blue cheeses include Gorgonzola from Italy, Stilton from England and Roquefort from France. Blue cheeses are always added with other ingredients because processing them alone makes the cheese look gray.

Butter

I use unsalted butter throughout the book. Many students ask me, "Why the unsalted butter?" I then ask them, "How much salt is in salted butter?" No one has the answer for me. I like to know exactly how much salt is in the food I am making. Unsalted butter allows me to control the salt by adding however much I think the recipe needs.

To process butter, make sure you cut the butter into small chunks and disperse them around the work bowl prior to processing. If you leave the butter in only a few chunks, they will just spin round and round without getting processed.

Eggs

The recipes in this book were tested using large eggs. Eggs are easier to separate when cold. After separating, allow eggs to come to room temperature before using. Leftover egg whites and yolks will keep for up to two days in a covered container in the refrigerator. Both can be frozen as well. Refrigerate eggs in the carton in which they came for up to a month.

In some areas you can purchase a pasteurized liquid egg product, not to be confused with liquid egg substitute. This is a great product for making recipes with raw eggs when you may have safety concerns. Please consult your medical professional prior to making or serving dishes with raw eggs if this is a concern for you.

Nuts

Nuts provide good nutritional value, including a generous amount of the good monounsaturated fat. But because of the high fat content, they have the corresponding high calories, too. They add flavor and texture to baked goods. Refrigerate or freeze shelled nuts that you won't use right away. For the best results, defrost and toast before proceeding with the recipe. To toast nuts, preheat oven to 350°F (180°C). Spread nuts on a baking sheet and bake for 10 to 12 minutes, checking a few times to make sure they don't burn. Let cool before processing.

To process nuts, use the metal blade and add a little of the dry ingredient, such as flour, from the recipe, otherwise you'll get nut butter. If you just want the nuts coarsely chopped, pulse a few times in the work bowl until the desired texture.

Chocolate

I am frequently asked the question, "Can I chop chocolate in my food processor?" The answer is yes. However, the heat from the machine melts the chocolate, so you may end up with chopped chocolate with melted pieces. I suggest that for ease you use a chocolate chopper instead (it looks like an ice pick with a row of six picks). A knife is not as desirable because it can become dull after a short time.

Produce

Fresh herbs

There is nothing like using fresh herbs in recipes. We are fortunate that most major grocery stores now carry fresh herbs year-round. Remove the herbs from the plastic container they may have come in. If the roots are still attached, remove them and the dirt. Wash the herbs with a light spray of cold water. Place the herbs in a herb spinner to dry, then roll in paper towels and store in a resealable plastic bag in your vegetable drawer.

When processing the herbs, peel the leaves off the bitter stems. Use the metal blade and pulse using the on/off button. For slightly chopped herbs, pulse only a few times. For a purée, let the motor run for 10 to 15 seconds.

Fruits and Vegetables

Processing: If the produce is round like an apple or an onion, discard the parts you would not normally eat, such as the core and peel. Then quarter the item and place around the work bowl. Pulse a few times until desired consistency. If you do not quarter the item first, your ingredient will just spin around the work bowl without getting chopped.

Slicing and shredding: Some fruits and vegetables are too large to fit into the feed tube, and then the pusher will be unable to activate the machine. I suggest that you slice your item to fit through the feed tube. Most often, this is about 2 inches (5 cm) long. If you have a round item, such as a mushroom, cut one end off with a knife to make it flat. Place the flat end first into the feed tube, then, using the plunger, press down while the machine is running.

Oil

I use a variety of good-quality oils in my recipes. Check the taste of the oil prior to use. Oils go rancid very quickly in a warm kitchen. When using olive oil for cooking I use regular olive oil rather than extra virgin because the heat destroys its healthy qualities. However, when using olive oil without heat, such as in salad dressings, I tend to use first press or extra virgin olive oil.

Yeast

Always check the package for the expiration date. I use quick-rising (instant) dry yeast, which has stronger yeast cells and produces faster rising dough.

Spices

I heard once years back that the shelf life of a spice was six months. You'd have to be cooking a great deal to use all of your spices if that were true. Purchase good-quality spices. Keep spices tightly sealed and store in a cool, dry, dark place, such as cupboard. I tend to use my spices within 12 to 18 months. Only purchase small amounts of spices that you do not use on a weekly basis.

Vanilla

Pure vanilla extract is created by soaking vanilla beans in bourbon or vodka and then aging the liquid. The flavor and aroma are unmistakable. Do not scrimp on the quality, nor delete vanilla from your recipes. Vanilla enhances all the other ingredients. In the past few years you may have noticed that vanilla has increased in price; however, your baked goods are worth it. Imitation vanilla is created with man-made products and barely resembles what it attempts to imitate. Despite being one-tenth the cost of the real thing, it is not worth substituting for pure vanilla extract.

Sources

Equipment and Services

George Geary, CCP
www.georgegeary.com
Author's website, full of recipes, tips, culinary tour information and teaching locations. Magic Line Pans are sold here.

Kitchen Art
765-497-3878 (Ships to U.S. only)
www.k-art.com
Privately owned cooking school and cookware shop outside of Purdue University. Full catalog of equipment.

Parrish's Cake Decorating Supplies
310-324-2253 or 800-736-8443
Magic Line Baking Pans, cheesecake pans, small hand tools.

The Cooking Studio
Winnipeg, Canada
204-896-5174
www.thecookingstudio.ca
Fine cookware school with classes and equipment.

The Kitchen Shoppe Inc.
800-391-2665 (Ships to U.S. only)
www.kitchenshoppe.com
Very large family-owned and -operated cookware shop with a large inventory.

Ingredients

Nielsen-Massey Vanillas
847-578-1550 or 800-575-7873
www.nielsenmassey.com
Fine producer of high-quality vanilla beans, pastes, extracts and more.

Extracts and Spices

Charles H. Baldwin & Sons
413-232-7785
www.baldwinextracts.com
Pure extracts, from anise to peppermint.

Penzey's Spices
262-785-7676 or 800-741-7787
www.penzeys.com
Family-owned and -operated premium spice company. Catalog is full of great facts. Retail stores in 14 states.

Appetizers

Salmon Herb Mousse on
    Stone Ground Crackers. 16

Shrimp Pâté with Leeks 17

Crab Feta Mushrooms 18

Thai Beef Skewers in Peanut Sauce 19

Mini Meatballs with Garlic Tomato Sauce 20

Grande Beef Nachos 22

Deviled Eggs with Caviar 23

Mini Chicken Puffs. 24

Crispy Chicken Cakes
    with Fresh Dill Mayonnaise 25

Fresh Bread Crumbs. 26

Savory Chicken Cheese Balls. 27

Black Bean Chipotle Dip 28

Hummus for a Crowd 29

Roasted Red Pepper Guacamole Dip 30

Tomatillo Onion Avocado Salsa. 31

Roasted Corn and Pepper Salsa 32

Peach Mango Salsa 33

Traditional Salsa. 34

Salmon Herb Mousse on Stone-Ground Crackers

**Makes ¾ cup
(175 mL)**

In my first hotel chef job I would make pounds and pounds of this flavorful mousse. It's fast, easy and elegant on toast points or crackers.

Tips

If the cream cheese is not softened, you can process it first and then add the salmon.

Mousse keeps well, covered and refrigerated, for up to 3 days.

Variation

I like to pipe the mixture on halved strawberries and serve on a large platter.

4 oz	smoked salmon	125 g
3 oz	cream cheese, softened	90 g
1 tsp	loosely packed tarragon leaves	5 mL
½ tsp	capers, divided	2 mL
24 to 36	stone-ground crackers	24 to 36
	Fresh tarragon sprigs	

1. In work bowl fitted with metal blade, add salmon and process until smooth, about 30 seconds. Add cream cheese and tarragon and process until smooth, about 10 seconds. Add ¼ tsp (1 mL) of the capers and pulse 8 times.

2. Place mousse into a pastry bag fitted with a star tip. Pipe onto stone ground crackers or spread with a knife. Top each with a sprig of tarragon and a few capers.

Shrimp Pâté with Leeks

I serve this pâté at every spring party I throw. It will make a great addition to your party, too.

Tips

Make sure you submerge the leeks in cool water when cleaning because there is sand in the reeds of the stalks.

Pâté keeps well, covered and refrigerated, for up to 3 days.

Variation

Add 2 cloves minced garlic to the pâté for a simple change in flavor.

2	leeks, white parts only, cut into quarters (about 1/2 cup/125 mL)	2
8 oz	cream cheese, softened	250 g
4 oz	cooked shrimp	125 g
2 tbsp	unsalted butter, softened	25 mL
2 tbsp	brandy	25 mL
Pinch	ground white pepper	Pinch
Pinch	salt	Pinch

1. In work bowl fitted with metal blade, add leeks and pulse until coarsely chopped, about 10 times. Transfer to a bowl and set aside.

2. In same work bowl fitted with metal blade, process cream cheese, shrimp, butter and brandy until smooth, about 2 minutes. With the motor running, add leeks, white pepper and salt through the feed tube and pulse until leeks are loosely incorporated, about 5 times.

Crab Feta Mushrooms

Hot and sizzling out of the oven, these mushrooms will be the hit of the party.

Tips

You can make the filling 1 day prior to serving. Transfer to a bowl. Cover and refrigerate. Let warm slightly before filling mushrooms.

When removing the stems from the mushrooms, check to see that they are fresh. Look under the cap, if the stem looks like it is becoming unattached or dark; your mushroom is getting old.

Variation

Use blue cheese or Stilton in place of the feta to give a sharp yet pleasant flavor to this appetizer.

- *Preheated broiler*
- *Baking sheet, lined with parchment paper*

1 lb	button mushrooms, stems removed and reserved	500 g
6 oz	lump canned crabmeat, drained, or frozen crabmeat, thawed	175 g
3 oz	feta cheese, crumbled	90 g
2	green onions, green part only, cut in half	2
1 tbsp	unsalted butter, softened	15 mL
1	clove garlic	1
¼ tsp	ground white pepper	1 mL
¼ tsp	salt	1 mL

1. Place mushrooms, caps down, on prepared baking sheet. Set aside.

2. In work bowl fitted with metal blade, process half of the mushroom stems, crabmeat, feta cheese, green onions, butter, garlic, white pepper and salt until smooth, 2 to 3 minutes. Discard remaining half of the mushroom stems.

3. Fill mushroom caps with cheese mixture. Broil under preheated broiler until cheese mixture starts to melt and bubble, about 3 minutes. Serve hot.

Thai Beef Skewers in Peanut Sauce

Finger foods and skewers are great appetizers for a cocktail party where people are eating and mingling.

Tips

Soak the skewers in water for at least 10 minutes prior to threading so they will not catch fire on the grill.

For a main dish, serve the beef skewers over a bed of rice.

You should be able to find all of the ingredients in your local grocery store in the international section.

Variation

You can use chicken in place of the beef.

- *Preheat grill to medium or oven to 400°F (200°C)*
- *13-by 9-inch (3 L) baking dish*
- *16 wooden skewers (see Tips, left)*

1 lb	boneless beef sirloin, sliced into ¼-inch (0.5 cm) strips	500 g
6	green onions, green part only, sliced in half	6
⅓ cup	peanut oil	75 mL
3 tbsp	freshly squeezed lemon juice	45 mL
2 tbsp	granulated sugar	25 mL
1 tbsp	sesame oil	15 mL
1 tbsp	hoisin sauce	15 mL
1 tbsp	low-sodium soy sauce (see Tip, page 94)	15 mL
1 tsp	dry mustard powder	5 mL
¼ tsp	ground white pepper	1 mL
¼ tsp	5-spice powder	1 mL
⅛ tsp	ground ginger	0.5 mL

1. Thread beef strips onto skewers and place in baking dish side by side in one layer. Set aside.

2. In work bowl fitted with metal blade, process green onions, peanut oil, lemon juice, sugar, sesame oil, hoisin sauce, soy sauce, dry mustard, white pepper, 5-spice powder and ginger until smooth, 2 to 3 minutes. Pour over beef. Cover and marinate in the refrigerator for 2 hours.

3. Grill over medium heat or bake in preheated oven, turning partway, until light brown, 20 to 25 minutes. Discard any excess marinade.

Mini Meatballs with Garlic Tomato Sauce

Serves 4

I like to serve these meatballs with little toothpicks as an appetizer for a party. The flavor is intense. You can also serve them as a main dish with a side of pasta.

Tip

Make sure the basil and parsley are washed and dried. I like to use a herb spinner to make sure they are as dry as can be.

Variations

You can substitute ground turkey for part or all of the pork.

- *Preheat oven to 350°F (180°C)*
- *13-by 9-inch (3 L) baking dish*

MEATBALLS

1 cup	Fresh Bread Crumbs (see recipe, page 26)	250 mL
½ cup	milk	125 mL
1	onion, cut into quarters	1
8 oz	ground beef	250 g
8 oz	ground pork	250 g
1	egg	1
½ tsp	ground allspice	2 mL
½ tsp	ground ginger	2 mL
⅛ tsp	salt	0.5 mL
1 tbsp	vegetable oil	15 mL

SAUCE

1 lb	Roma tomatoes (7 to 9 tomatoes)	500 g
6	cloves garlic	6
⅓ cup	fresh basil leaves, washed and stemmed (see Tip, left)	75 mL
2 tbsp	Italian parsley	25 mL
⅓ cup	olive oil	75 mL

1. *Meatballs:* Place bread crumbs in a large bowl. Add milk and let it absorb.

2. In work bowl fitted with metal blade, add onion and process until chopped, about 10 seconds. Add to bread crumbs with ground beef, ground pork, egg, allspice, ginger and salt. Blend together. Shape mixture into about 24 1-inch (2.5 cm) meatballs.

3. Heat vegetable oil in a frying pan over medium heat. Add meatballs and sauté until light brown, 3 to 4 minutes. Place in baking dish, cover and bake in preheated oven until no longer pink inside, 20 to 25 minutes. Drain off any excess oil.

4. *Sauce:* Cut tomatoes in half, widthwise. Remove cores and squeeze out excess seeds and juices. Transfer to clean work bowl fitted with metal blade. Add garlic cloves, basil and parsley and pulse until chunky but not smooth, about 10 times. With the motor running, gradually add olive oil through the feed tube and process until smooth. Transfer sauce to a saucepan over medium heat and bring to a simmer. Toss meatballs with warm sauce.

Grande Beef Nachos

When you get a crowd over you need to serve something fast and hearty. This dish can be put together in just a few minutes.

Tip

Do not place the hot meat mixture over the corn chips until you are ready to microwave. It will make your chips soggy.

Variations

Use ground sausage (casings removed) in place of the ground beef to add a little zip.

You can also make this in the oven. Place under preheated broiler until cheese melts, 2 to 5 minutes.

1		bag (12 oz/375 g) tortilla chips	1
8 oz		Cheddar cheese, cut into chunks	250 g
8 oz		Monterey Jack cheese, cut into chunks	250 g
1		onion, cut into quarters	1
1		can (14 to 19 oz/398 to 540 mL) pinto or black beans, drained and rinsed	1
1 tsp		chili powder	5 mL
1 tsp		paprika	5 mL
3/4 tsp		salt	4 mL
3/4 tsp		dried onion flakes	4 mL
1/4 tsp		cayenne pepper	1 mL
1/4 tsp		onion powder	1 mL
1/8 tsp		ground oregano	0.5 mL
8 oz		lean ground beef	250 g
1/4 cup		sour cream	50 mL

1. On a microwave-safe platter, place chips in a single layer. Set aside.

2. In work bowl fitted with shredding blade, shred Cheddar and Monterey Jack cheeses. Transfer to a bowl and set aside.

3. Replace shredding blade with metal blade. With the motor running, drop onion though the feed tube and process until finely chopped. Into the work bowl, add beans, chili powder, paprika, salt, onion flakes, cayenne pepper, onion powder and oregano and process until smooth, 2 to 3 minutes.

4. In a large skillet over medium heat, cook ground beef until no longer pink, 10 to 15 minutes. Drain off fat. Add bean mixture and cook, stirring, until hot.

5. Spoon beef mixture over chips. Sprinkle cheese mixture over top. Microwave for 20 seconds or until cheese is bubbling. Garnish with sour cream.

Deviled Eggs with Caviar

Makes 12

Little beads of caviar offset the bright yellow of these stuffed eggs.

Tips

You can make the egg mixture 1 or 2 days prior to your party and pipe the filling into the egg whites the day of the party. Cover with plastic wrap and refrigerate until just before serving. Place the caviar eggs on top right before serving.

Use ½ tsp (2 mL) prepared mustard in place of the dry mustard powder.

Variation

For an Asian flavor, I like to substitute ⅛ tsp (0.5 mL) 5-spice powder for the curry powder.

● *Large bowl of ice water*

6	eggs	6
⅓ cup	Traditional Mayonnaise (see recipe, page 36) or store-bought	75 mL
2	strips cooked bacon	2
¼ tsp	dry mustard powder (see Tips, left)	1 mL
⅛ tsp	curry powder	0.5 mL
Pinch	salt	Pinch
⅛ tsp	caviar	0.5 mL

1. Place eggs on the bottom of a saucepan in a single layer and add enough cold water to cover by 1 inch (2.5 cm). Bring to a boil over high heat. Remove from heat and without draining the water, cover and let stand for 10 minutes. With a slotted spoon, carefully place eggs in a large bowl filled with ice water. Let cool completely for 5 minutes. Remove eggshells under cool running water. Cut eggs lengthwise and carefully remove yolk, keeping egg white intact. Set egg white halves on a plate.

2. In work bowl fitted with metal blade, process egg yolks, mayonnaise, bacon, dry mustard, curry powder and salt until smooth, about 30 seconds. Taste and add more salt, if desired.

3. Using a pastry bag fitted with a star tip or using a spoon, pipe or spoon mixture into egg white halves. Top with a few caviar eggs.

Mini Chicken Puffs

Makes 32 puffs

Perfect for large get-togethers! You only have to make one batch to feed a crowd.

Tips

It's important to always use cooked items, such as the chicken, in puff pastry because the cooking time does not allow raw meats to cook fully.

If you have a smaller package of puff pastry, the pastry may be thinner, but will still work. If the pastry feels too thin to enclose filling, you may need to use a little less chicken mixture for each square.

Variation

Mini Vegetarian Puffs: Replace the chicken with 8 oz (250 g) portobello mushrooms that have been sliced with the slicing blade.

- *Preheat oven to 425°F (220°C)*
- *2 baking sheets, lined with parchment paper*

1	package (18 oz/560 g) puff pastry, thawed (see Tips, left)	1
	All-purpose flour, for rolling pastry	
4 oz	Cheddar cheese, cut into chunks	125 g
8 oz	cooked chicken (see Tips, left)	250 g
2	green onions, green part only, cut in half	2
1/4 cup	Smoked Chili Sauce (see recipe, page 174) or store-bought	50 mL

1. Working with one half of pastry, on a lightly floured board, roll pastry into a 12-inch (30 cm) square. Using a pizza cutter, cut equally, horizontally and vertically so you end up with 4 strips by 4 strips to make 16 squares. Set aside.

2. In work bowl fitted with shredding blade, shred cheese. Transfer to a bowl and set aside.

3. Replace shredding blade with metal blade. Add chicken, green onions and chili sauce and pulse until mixture is chunky, 5 to 8 times. Place 1 tbsp (15 mL) of the mixture on center of each rectangle. Top with 1½ tsp (7 mL) of the cheese. Starting with two opposite corners of one square of pastry, fold in toward the center to meet above filling. With remaining corners, fold up to meet in the center and squeeze edges together to seal (like a dim sum dumpling). If pastry seems dry, lightly brush edges with water before folding to ensure a good seal. Place on prepared baking sheets about 2 inches (5 cm) apart. Repeat with remaining pastry squares and filling to make 32 puffs.

4. Bake in preheated oven until light brown and puffed up, 14 to 18 minutes. Serve warm or cold with Chipotle Mayonnaise (see recipe, page 38).

Crispy Chicken Cakes with Fresh Dill Mayonnaise

These herbed cakes are packed with so much flavor and pizzazz that every time I make them as an appetizer I'm asked to make them as a main dish.

Tips

You can form the patties and refrigerate them up to 3 days ahead. Coat with bread crumbs when you are ready to use them. Allow for a few extra minutes on each side when cooking them.

You can purchase cooked chickens at most grocery stores to reduce your preparation time.

Variation

Herbed Seafood Cakes: Substitute 3 cups (750 mL) chopped cooked or thawed frozen crab for the chicken.

12 oz	cooked chicken	375 g
1 cup	Fresh Bread Crumbs (see recipe, page 26), divided	250 mL
¼ cup	Traditional Mayonnaise (see recipe, page 36), Fresh Dill Mayonnaise (see recipe, page 37) or store-bought	50 mL
1	egg	1
2 tsp	prepared mustard	10 mL
⅓ cup	roasted red peppers (about 1 small)	75 mL
½	red onion, cut into quarters (about ⅓ cup/75 mL)	½
2 tbsp	olive oil	25 mL
	Fresh Dill Mayonnaise (see recipe, page 37)	

1. In work bowl fitted with metal blade, process cooked chicken, ½ cup (125 mL) of the bread crumbs, mayonnaise, egg, mustard, red peppers and onion until almost smooth, about 30 seconds. Mixture will be tacky. With moistened hands, form into 10 patties if making appetizers or 6 patties if making a main course. Coat with remaining bread crumbs. Discard any excess crumbs.

2. Heat half of the olive oil in a frying pan over medium heat. Add patties, in batches, and fry until light brown, 3 minutes per side, adding more oil as necessary. Serve with Fresh Dill Mayonnaise.

Fresh Bread Crumbs

*Many recipes call for
bread crumbs, and if
you have extra pieces
of bread you can make
your own. I recall in
France we had so much
bread left after a few
days that I wouldn't let
anyone eat it because
I wanted to make
bread crumbs.*

Tip

Make sure you tear the
bread up prior to baking
so the bread dries faster
and evenly.

Variation

Add 1 tsp (5 mL) Italian
herb seasonings when
processing for Italian
bread crumbs.

• *Preheat oven to 300°F (150°C)*
• *Baking sheet, lined with parchment paper*

4	slices French or Italian bread, each 1 inch (2.5 cm) thick, torn into small pieces	4

1. Place bread on prepared baking sheet and toast in preheated oven for 5 minutes. Turn and continue to bake until very light brown and dried, 5 minutes more. Remove and let dry at room temperature for about 1 hour.

2. In work bowl fitted with metal blade, process toasted bread pieces until fine crumbs. Freeze in a resealable plastic freezer bag for up to 3 months.

Savory Chicken Cheese Balls

These cheese balls are so creamy and rich. I love serving them with crackers or carrot sticks.

Tips

To toast almonds: Place almonds in a dry nonstick skillet over medium heat and toast, stirring constantly, until golden brown, 3 to 4 minutes.

You can use lower-fat cream cheese and sour cream without sacrificing flavor or texture.

Variation

Use 2 fresh apricots in place of the grapes.

½ cup	toasted sliced almonds (see Tips, left)	125 mL
2	packages (each 8 oz/250 g) cream cheese, softened	2
1 lb	cooked chicken	500 g
1 cup	seedless grapes	250 mL
6	green onions, green part only, cut in half (about ½ cup/125 mL)	6
2 tbsp	sour cream	25 mL
1 tsp	curry powder	5 mL
1 tsp	seasoned salt	5 mL

1. In work bowl fitted with metal blade, add almonds and pulse until finely ground, about 10 times. Transfer to a small bowl and set aside.

2. In same work bowl fitted with metal blade, process cream cheese until smooth. Add chicken, grapes, green onions, sour cream, curry powder and seasoned salt and process until smooth, 2 to 3 minutes. Divide mixture between 2 pieces of plastic wrap and form each into 2 balls, wrapping to seal. Refrigerate until firm, about 30 minutes or for up to 3 days.

3. Just before serving, remove plastic wrap and roll balls in chopped almonds. Place on a serving dish.

Black Bean Chipotle Dip

A colleague of mine, Cathi Hofsetter, makes this wonderful dip. I added chipotle pepper to give it a little kick. Serve with crackers, chips or toast points.

Tips

Dip will keep, covered and refrigerated, for up to 1 week. The flavors get stronger after a day or two.

Make sure the cilantro is completely dry after cleaning. Otherwise the dip may be too watery. Dry herbs in an herb spinner.

Variation

I like to substitute pinto beans for the black beans for a lighter looking dip.

1	can (14 to 19 oz/398 to 540 mL) black beans, drained and rinsed	1
12 oz	cream cheese, softened	375 g
1/3 cup	roasted red peppers (about 1 small)	75 mL
1/2 to 1	chipotle pepper in adobo sauce, drained	1/2 to 1
1 tbsp	fresh cilantro leaves (see Tips, left)	15 mL
1 tbsp	taco seasoning	15 mL
1 tsp	freshly squeezed lime juice	5 mL

1. In work bowl fitted with metal blade, process black beans, cream cheese, red peppers, chipotle pepper to taste, cilantro, taco seasoning and lime juice until smooth, about 2 minutes. Transfer to a serving dish.

Hummus for a Crowd

*I believe if you're making
a dip you should make
enough for a crowd
because you'll want to
snack on this hummus
for days after your party.*

Tips

Store hummus, covered
and refrigerated, for up
to 3 days.

If the hummus is too
thick after a few days
you can thin it with
additional lemon juice
before serving.

Tahini paste should be
stored in the refrigerator.
Taste it before use. It
should have a clean
nutty taste and not taste
like rancid sesame seeds.

Variation

Add 2 tsp (10 mL) fresh
mint leaves with parsley.

1	can (16 or 19 oz/454 or 540 mL) chickpeas, drained and rinsed	1
1	clove garlic	1
1/3 cup	tahini paste	75 mL
1/2 cup	freshly squeezed lemon juice (approx.)	125 mL
1 tbsp	Italian parsley leaves	15 mL
1/8 tsp	ground cumin	0.5 mL

1. In work bowl fitted with metal blade, process chickpeas, garlic and tahini paste until smooth, about 30 seconds. With the motor running, drizzle lemon juice through the feed tube and process until desired consistency. Add parsley and cumin and process until smooth. Serve with cracker bread or flatbreads.

Roasted Red Pepper Guacamole Dip

Makes 1½ cups (375 mL)

I like to use this recipe as a sandwich spread on crusty French bread.

Tip

Make sure you do not overprocess the mixture or you will have soup.

Variation

Add 4 seeded Roma tomatoes that have been processed into the dip if you have additional guests show up.

1	red onion, cut into quarters (about ⅔ cup/150 mL)	1
2	jalapeño peppers, seeded	2
½ cup	fresh cilantro leaves (see Tips, page 28)	125 mL
3	avocados, peeled and pitted, cut in half	3
½ cup	roasted red peppers	125 mL

1. In work bowl fitted with metal blade, pulse red onion and jalapeño peppers until chopped, about 8 times. Add cilantro and pulse 5 times. Add avocados and red peppers and process until chopped, about 10 seconds.

2. Transfer to a bowl. Cover and refrigerate for at least 1 hour or for up to 1 day. Serve chilled.

Tomatillo Onion Avocado Salsa

Makes 2½ cups (625 mL)

When I have parties I like to serve two different colors of salsa. This green flavorful salsa takes only a few minutes to blend together. For other different-colored salsas to serve with it see Roasted Corn and Pepper Salsa (page 32), Peach Mango Salsa (page 33) or Traditional Salsa (page 34).

Tip

Prior to processing, make sure you run the tomatillos under water to wash the stickiness off after you have removed the papery skins from the green skins.

Variation

Add ¼ tsp (1 mL) hot pepper sauce to the mixture to add more zip.

½	red onion, cut into quarters (about ⅓ cup/75 mL)	½
1 lb	tomatillos, husked, rinsed and cut into quarters (about 15) (see Tip, left)	500 g
1	avocado, peeled and pitted, cut in half	1
1	serrano chile	1
1 cup	loosely packed fresh cilantro leaves	250 mL
2 tbsp	freshly squeezed lime juice	25 mL
1 tsp	salt	5 mL

1. In work bowl fitted with metal blade, add onion and pulse until chunky, about 10 times. Place into a strainer and rinse with water. Drain well. Return to work bowl. Add tomatillos, avocado, serrano chile, cilantro, lime juice and salt and pulse until the desired texture is achieved, about 20 times. Some people like it chunky so the salsa can stay on a chip while others prefer it smooth. You decide. This is also great as a topping on burgers.

Roasted Corn and Pepper Salsa

Makes about 5 cups (1.25 L)

This hot and spicy salsa is made on the grill. Serve with chips or with chicken or fish. I like serving it with margaritas.

Tips

Do not run water over the chiles to try to loosen the skins. If the skins do not come off easily, you need to let them steam longer in the plastic bag. If you use water over the chiles, you will wash the flavor off.

Place the corn, tomatoes and chiles under the broiler until the skins bubble and the corn is browned, about 10 minutes.

Variations

You can use cherry tomatoes in place of Roma and you won't have to seed them.

Use a combination of 6 oz (175 g) jalapeño or hot banana peppers and 6 oz (175 g) poblano or cubanelle peppers if you can't find New Mexico chiles.

● *Preheat barbecue to medium*

6	ears corn	6
2 tbsp	olive oil, divided	25 mL
1 lb	Roma tomatoes (7 to 9 tomatoes)	500 g
12 oz	New Mexico or Anaheim chiles (10 to 12 chiles)	375 g
1	onion, cut into quarters	1
1/4 cup	cider vinegar	50 mL
1 tsp	granulated sugar	5 mL
1/2 tsp	dried oregano leaves	2 mL
1/4 tsp	salt	1 mL

1. Remove husks from corn cobs. Brush 1 tbsp (15 mL) olive oil on all sides and place on preheated grill. Brush tomatoes and chiles with remaining oil and place on grill. Grill, turning to brown all sides, about 20 minutes. When the corn starts to brown, remove from heat and let cool. When chiles and tomatoes start to blister, place in a plastic bag to sweat for 20 minutes.

2. Slice corn from cobs and place in a large bowl. Peel skins from sweated chiles. Cut chiles in half and scrape out seeds and membranes.

3. In work bowl fitted with metal blade, pulse chiles until chunky, about 10 times. Add to corn.

4. Peel skins off sweated tomatoes, remove cores and cut in half. Try removing all of the seeds. Place in same work bowl fitted with metal blade and pulse until smooth, about 10 times. Add to corn mixture.

5. In same work bowl fitted with metal blade, pulse onion, vinegar, sugar, oregano and salt until chunky, about 10 times. Add to corn mixture. Stir to combine. Let rest for 30 minutes.

Hummus for a Crowd (page 29), and
Roasted Corn and Pepper Salsa (page 32)

Peach Mango Salsa

As well as with chips for a great-tasting dip, this sweet and fruity salsa can be used on top of fish and chicken.

Tips

Salsa keeps well, covered and refrigerated, for up to 1 week.

If you use thin-skinned peaches you will not need to peel them prior to use.

Variation

If you would like a less spicy salsa, omit the cayenne pepper.

I	piece (½ inch/I cm) fresh ginger	I
2	large peaches, pitted and cut into quarters (see Tips, left)	2
I	large mango, peeled, pitted and cut into quarters	I
I tbsp	freshly squeezed lime juice	15 mL
½ tsp	cayenne pepper	2 mL
½ tsp	salt	2 mL

1. With a garlic press or ginger grater, press juice from ginger so you have ½ tsp (2 mL). Transfer to a bowl.

2. In work bowl fitted with metal blade, pulse peaches and mango until chunky, 8 to 10 times. Transfer to bowl with ginger juice. Add lime juice, cayenne pepper and salt. Toss together.

Green Salad with Thousand Island Dressing (page 47)

Traditional Salsa

This is an all-purpose salsa. Great with chips, grilled meats or tacos.

Tips

Salsa keeps well, covered and refrigerated, for 1 week.

When seeding the chiles wear rubber gloves and discard the seeds. If any of the chile juice gets on your fingers and you rub your eyes you will feel it.

Variation

You can replace the serrano chiles with jalapeño peppers for a hotter flavor.

1	onion, cut into quarters	1
1 lb	Roma tomatoes, cored, cut in half and seeded (7 to 9 tomatoes)	500 g
2	serrano chiles, cut in half and seeded	2
¼ cup	loosely packed cilantro leaves	50 mL
2 tbsp	freshly squeezed lime juice	25 mL
2 tsp	granulated sugar	10 mL
1 tsp	salt (approx.)	5 mL

1. In work bowl fitted with metal blade, pulse onion until finely chopped, 10 to 12 times. Place into a strainer and rinse with water. Drain well. Transfer to a bowl and set aside.

2. In same work bowl fitted with metal blade, pulse tomatoes, chiles and cilantro until desired consistency, 15 to 20 times.

3. Add tomato mixture to drained onions. Add lime juice, sugar and salt to taste. Let stand for at least 1 hour prior to use.

Salads and Salad Dressings

Traditional Mayonnaise 36

Fresh Dill Mayonnaise 37

Chipotle Mayonnaise 38

Tarragon Dill Butter 39

Honey Butter 40

Blue Cheese Peanut Coleslaw 41

Roasted Chicken Garlic Salad Sandwiches 42

Egg Salad Spread 43

Pepper Pasta Salad 44

Creamy French Salad Dressing 46

Thousand Island Dressing 47

Blue Cheese Peppercorn Dressing 48

Avocado Tamarind Cashew Dressing 49

Raspberry Vinaigrette 50

Traditional Mayonnaise

*If you've never tasted
fresh homemade
mayonnaise you are
in for a treat. Fresh
mayonnaise is so silky.
It's nothing like its
stepsister in the jar.*

Tips
This recipe contains raw
egg yolks. If the food
safety of raw eggs is a
concern for you, use
pasteurized eggs in the
shell or pasteurized liquid
whole eggs instead.

If egg yolks are not
processed for the full
2 minutes they will not
emulsify correctly when
the oil is incorporated.

Mayonnaise keeps well,
covered and refrigerated,
for 3 to 5 days. If using
pasteurized eggs, it will
keep for up to 2 weeks.

Variation

Try flavored oils in place
of the plain vegetable oil
to enhance your dishes.

2	egg yolks, at room temperature, or ¼ cup (50 mL) pasteurized eggs (liquid or in the shell) (see Tips, left)	2
2 tbsp	white wine vinegar	25 mL
1 tsp	dry mustard powder	5 mL
1 tsp	sea salt	5 mL
1 tsp	granulated sugar	5 mL
½ tsp	ground white pepper	2 mL
1 cup	vegetable oil	250 mL

1. In work bowl fitted with metal blade, process egg yolks, vinegar, dry mustard, sea salt, sugar and white pepper until smooth, for 2 minutes (see Tips, left). With the processor running, slowly drizzle oil through the small hole in the feed tube until it has been incorporated into the mayonnaise (see Tips, page 37).

2. When all of the oil is drizzled into egg mixture, remove processor lid and, with a rubber spatula, scrape down the sides and bottom, which sometimes collect residue, as necessary to incorporate all of the mixture. Replace lid and process for about 15 seconds.

Fresh Dill Mayonnaise

*I love using this spread
with roasted chicken
sandwiches.*

Tips
Mayonnaise keeps well,
covered and refrigerated,
for 3 to 5 days. If using
pasteurized eggs, it will
keep for up to 2 weeks.

If your food processor
has a feed tube with the
drip feature (a small hole
in the bottom of the
tube), fill the tube with
oil and let oil drizzle in,
refilling the tube with
oil as it drains until all
is incorporated. If not,
pour a thin, steady stream
through the tube to make
sure oil gets emulsified
properly. Adding the oil
too quickly can cause the
mayonnaise to separate.

I do not advise making
a double batch of this
mayonnaise unless you
use it within the week.
The dill will turn dark
after a week.

Variation

Try the same amount
of rosemary in place
of the dill for another
herb flavor.

3	egg yolks, at room temperature, or ⅓ cup (75 mL) pasteurized eggs (liquid or in the shell) (see Tips, page 36)	3
3 tbsp	sherry vinegar	45 mL
2 tsp	mustard seeds	10 mL
2 tsp	sea salt	10 mL
1½ tsp	granulated sugar	7 mL
1 tsp	ground white pepper	5 mL
1 cup	peanut oil	250 mL
2 tbsp	loosely packed fresh dill	25 mL

1. In work bowl fitted with metal blade, process egg yolks, vinegar, mustard seeds, sea salt, sugar and white pepper until smooth, for 2 minutes (see Tips, page 36). With the motor running, slowly drizzle oil through the small hole in the feed tube until it has been incorporated into the mayonnaise (see Tips, left).

2. When all of the oil is drizzled into egg mixture, remove processor lid and, with a rubber spatula, scrape down the sides and bottom, which sometimes collect residue, as necessary to incorporate all of the mixture. Add fresh dill. Replace lid and process for about 15 seconds.

Chipotle Mayonnaise

A dollop of this tasty mayonnaise on the side of any meat dish will enhance the flavor.

Tips

This recipe contains raw egg yolks. If the food safety of raw eggs is a concern for you, use pasteurized eggs in the shell or pasteurized liquid whole eggs instead.

If egg yolks are not processed for the full 2 minutes they will not emulsify correctly when the oil is incorporated.

Mayonnaise keeps well, covered and refrigerated, for 3 to 5 days. If using pasteurized eggs, it will keep for up to 2 weeks.

If you have any of the adobo sauce left from the chiles you can fold it into the mayonnaise to make a great dip for chips.

Variation

You can add $\frac{1}{8}$ tsp (0.5 mL) cayenne pepper for an added spice.

2	egg yolks, at room temperature, or $\frac{1}{4}$ cup (50 mL) pasteurized eggs (liquid or in the shell) (see Tips, left)	2
2 tbsp	white wine vinegar	25 mL
1 tsp	dry mustard powder	5 mL
1 tsp	sea salt	5 mL
1 tsp	granulated sugar	5 mL
$\frac{1}{2}$ tsp	ground white pepper	2 mL
$\frac{1}{4}$ tsp	ground nutmeg	1 mL
$\frac{3}{4}$ cup	vegetable oil	175 mL
2	chipotle peppers in adobo sauce, drained and seeded	2

1. In work bowl fitted with metal blade, process egg yolks, vinegar, dry mustard, sea salt, sugar, white pepper and ground nutmeg until smooth, for 2 minutes (see Tips, left). With the motor running, slowly drizzle oil through the small hole in the feed tube until it has been incorporated into the mayonnaise (see Tips, page 37).

2. When all of the oil is drizzled into egg mixture, remove processor lid and, with a rubber spatula, scrape down the sides and bottom, which sometimes collect residue, as necessary to incorporate all of the mixture. Add chipotle peppers. Replace the lid and process for about 10 seconds.

Tarragon Dill Butter

Makes 1 cup (250 mL)

When dining in France you'll always get a flavorful butter on top of your vegetables or meats. I like to make this butter for breads and corn muffins.

Tip

Make sure the butter is softened prior to using or it will not blend with the herbs.

Variation

Substitute ½ tsp (2 mL) loosely packed fresh thyme leaves for the dill for a different flavor.

● *Baking sheet, lined with parchment paper*

1 cup	unsalted butter, softened (see Tip, left)	250 mL
1 tsp	loosely packed fresh tarragon leaves	5 mL
½ tsp	loosely packed fresh dill	2 mL
¼ tsp	sea salt	1 mL

1. In work bowl fitted with metal blade, process butter, tarragon, dill and sea salt until smooth, about 3 minutes.

2. Place butter mixture into a pastry bag fitted with a star tip and pipe rosettes onto parchment paper. Or place in small individual ramekins. Refrigerate until firm, about 30 minutes. Remove rosettes from parchment with an offset spatula. Place in a freezer bag and freeze for up to 1 month.

Honey Butter

**Makes 1½ cups
(375 mL)**

When I was the pastry chef for Disney this was one of the most popular butters. Serve it with cornbread as we did.

Tips

Butter keeps in a covered dish in the refrigerator for up to 3 weeks.

Make sure your butter is unsalted or you will have salty tasting honey butter.

Variation

Try using a different-flavored honey such as lavender or clove.

1 cup	unsalted butter, softened (see Tips, left)	250 mL
½ cup	liquid honey	125 mL
1 tsp	ground cinnamon	5 mL
½ tsp	ground nutmeg	2 mL

1. In work bowl fitted with metal blade, process butter, honey, cinnamon and nutmeg until smooth, about 2 minutes. Place in small dish for serving.

Blue Cheese Peanut Coleslaw

The rich bite of the blue cheese with the creamy peanut dressing makes this coleslaw a picnic favorite.

Tips

Makes sure both the carrots and cabbage are chopped small enough to fit through the feed tube.

Salad keeps well, covered and refrigerated, for up to 3 days.

To speed up the process of making this salad, have all your vegetables cut and ready.

Variation

If you have spare garlic on hand add 2 crushed cloves to the onions for added flavor.

½ cup	Traditional Mayonnaise (see recipe, page 36) or store-bought	125 mL
1 tsp	freshly squeezed lemon juice	5 mL
Pinch	freshly ground black pepper	Pinch
Pinch	salt	Pinch
Pinch	granulated sugar	Pinch
1	onion, cut into quarters	1
1	green pepper, seeded and cut into quarters	1
2	large carrots, coarsely chopped (see Tips, left)	2
12 oz	cabbage, cut into wedges (about ½ head) (see Tips, left)	375 g
4 oz	blue cheese, crumbled	125 g
1¼ cups	unsalted roasted peanuts, crushed (about 8 oz/250 g)	300 mL

1. In a large salad bowl, whisk mayonnaise, lemon juice, pepper, salt and sugar until combined. Set aside.

2. In work bowl fitted with metal blade, process onion and green pepper until very finely chopped, about 30 seconds. Place in salad bowl.

3. Replace metal blade with shredding blade. With the motor running, add carrots through the feed tube and shred. Remove from work bowl. Add carrots to salad bowl.

4. Replace shredding blade with slicing blade. With the motor running, add cabbage through the feed tube and slice. Place in salad bowl.

5. Stir all ingredients together. Add blue cheese and roasted peanuts, making sure everything is well coated. Cover and place in the refrigerator for at least 1 hour prior to serving.

Roasted Chicken Garlic Salad Sandwiches

I tend to make this with any leftover chicken purchased from the grocery store deli section. This recipe uses an entire chicken, but you can adjust the recipe for your needs.

Tips

Spread keeps well, covered and refrigerated, for up to 3 days.

Do not overprocess the chicken spread or you'll get a creamy consistency. Avoid this by pulsing the mixture as instructed.

Variation

If using store-bought mayonnaise add 2 tbsp (25 mL) fresh dill to the mixture.

2	firm tomatoes	2
½	red onion, cut into quarters	½
3 lbs	prepared deli chicken, deboned	1.5 kg
3 oz	cream cheese, softened	90 g
3	cloves garlic	3
⅓ cup	Fresh Dill Mayonnaise (see recipe, page 37) or store-bought (see Variation, left)	75 mL
¼ tsp	freshly ground black pepper	1 mL
¼ tsp	salt	1 mL
12	slices whole wheat bread, toasted	12

1. In work bowl fitted with slicing blade, with the motor running, add tomatoes through the feed tube using the pusher with firm pressure and slice. Set aside.

2. Replace slicing blade with metal blade. Add onion and process until finely chopped. Add chicken, cream cheese and garlic and pulse until coarsely chopped, about 6 times. Add mayonnaise, black pepper and salt and pulse about 5 times. Divide spread among six bread slices. Top with tomato slices and remaining bread slices.

Egg Salad Spread

**Makes 2 cups
(500 mL)**

When I have an abundance of colored eggs after Easter, I tend to make this spread so I will have lunch for a few days.

Tips

Spread keeps, covered and refrigerated, for up to 3 days.

You can hard-boil the eggs a few days prior to use.

Variation

If you like a chunky texture in your spread just pulse the mixture instead of processing it to the desired texture.

● *Large bowl of ice water*

8	eggs	8
1/3 cup	Traditional Mayonnaise (see recipe, page 36) or store-bought	75 mL
4 oz	cooked ham or salami	125 g
1 tsp	prepared mustard	5 mL
1 tsp	loosely packed fresh dill	5 mL
1/8 tsp	ground nutmeg	0.5 mL
Pinch	salt	Pinch

1. Place eggs on the bottom of a saucepan in a single layer and add enough cold water to cover by 1 inch (2.5 cm). Bring to a boil over high heat. Remove from heat and without draining the water, cover and let stand for 10 minutes. With a slotted spoon, carefully place eggs in a large bowl filled with ice water. Let cool completely for 5 minutes. Remove eggshells under cool running water. Let eggs come to room temperature.

2. In work bowl fitted with metal blade, process eggs, mayonnaise, ham, mustard, dill, nutmeg and salt until smooth, about 30 seconds. Taste and add more salt, if desired.

Pepper Pasta Salad

This is a perfect salad for a picnic or a large gathering. You'll have plenty of leftovers for another meal.

Tips

Salad keeps, covered and refrigerated, for up to 1 week.

Do not "wash" the cooked pasta with water or it will stick. Coat with the olive oil as directed.

Variation

Try adding 8 oz (250 g) chopped meat, such as ham, salami or turkey, for a main entrée salad.

8 oz	multicolored corkscrew pasta	250 g
⅔ cup	extra virgin olive oil, divided	150 mL
3	green onions, green part only, cut in half	3
½	green bell pepper, seeded and halved	½
½	red bell pepper, seeded and halved	½
½	yellow bell pepper, seeded and halved	½
½ cup	packed fresh basil leaves, stems removed	125 mL
6 oz	Parmesan cheese, cut into chunks	175 g
2 tbsp	balsamic vinegar	25 mL
1½ tsp	Dijon mustard	7 mL
3	cloves garlic	3
½ tsp	granulated sugar	2 mL
Pinch	salt	Pinch
Pinch	hot pepper flakes	Pinch
2	carrots, coarsely chopped	2

1. In a large pot of boiling salted water, cook pasta until al dente, 7 to 12 minutes for dried, 3 to 6 minutes for fresh. Drain well and place in a large bowl. Add ¼ cup (50 mL) of the olive oil and toss to coat. Set aside and let cool to room temperature, occasionally stirring pasta to coat evenly.

2. In work bowl fitted with metal blade, pulse green onions, green, red and yellow peppers and basil 10 times. Add to pasta and toss.

3. In same work bowl, with the motor running, add Parmesan cheese through the feed tube and process until grated. Add vinegar, mustard, garlic, sugar, salt and hot pepper flakes and process until smooth, about 2 minutes. With the motor running, slowly drizzle remaining olive oil through the feed tube until it has been incorporated into the dressing. Pour over pasta salad.

4. In clean work bowl fitted with shredding blade, with the motor running, add carrots through the feed tube and shred. Add to pasta and toss. Let stand for at least 30 minutes prior to serving for the flavors to develop.

Creamy French Salad Dressing

*I never purchase bottled
dressing because I
dislike the manufactured
taste. Plus, when you
make it yourself you
know what's going
into it.*

Tips

Dressing keeps, covered
and refrigerated, for up
to 2 weeks. Warm to
room temperature before
serving.

Use dried herbs in this
recipe because they are
more intense and keep
better after a few days
than the fresh would.

Variation

For a richer flavor try
1 cup (250 mL) peanut
oil in place of the
vegetable.

4 oz	Parmesan cheese, cut into chunks	125 g
¾ cup	white wine vinegar	175 mL
⅔ cup	tomato paste	150 mL
½ cup	warm water	125 mL
3 tbsp	granulated sugar	45 mL
2 tsp	salt	10 mL
1 tsp	dried basil leaves (see Tips, left)	5 mL
1 tsp	dried tarragon leaves	5 mL
1 tsp	onion flakes	5 mL
1 cup	vegetable oil	250 mL

1. In work bowl fitted with metal blade, with the motor
   running, add Parmesan cheese through the feed tube
   and process until grated. With motor continuing to
   run, slowly pour vinegar, tomato paste and warm water
   through feed tube and process until blended. Remove
   lid and add sugar, salt, basil, tarragon and onion flakes,
   then cover and process until incorporated.

2. With the motor running, slowly drizzle oil through the
   feed tube until it has been incorporated into dressing.

Thousand Island Dressing

Makes 1½ cups (375 mL)

This is the dressing that some fast food establishments call "secret sauce." It was first created at a resort hotel in the Thousand Island area of upstate New York in the early 20th century.

Tips

Dressing keeps, covered and refrigerated, for up to 3 days.

You can use 2 tbsp (25 mL) sweet pickle relish if you are out of pickles.

Variation

Use 1 cup (250 mL) Chipotle Mayonnaise (see recipe, page 38) in place of the regular mayonnaise for a smoky flavor.

● *Large bowl of ice water*

I	egg	I
I cup	Traditional Mayonnaise (see recipe, page 36) or store-bought	250 mL
¼ cup	Smoked Chili Sauce (see recipe, page 174) or store-bought	50 mL
¼ cup	pimento-stuffed olives	50 mL
I	sweet pickle, cut in half (about 2 tbsp/25 mL)	I
I ½ tsp	onion flakes	7 mL
I ½ tsp	freshly squeezed lemon juice	7 mL
I tsp	dried parsley	5 mL
Pinch	salt	Pinch
Pinch	freshly ground black pepper	Pinch

1. Place egg in a small saucepan and add about 1 inch (2.5 cm) water to cover. Bring to a boil over high heat. Remove from heat and without draining the water, cover and let stand for 8 to 10 minutes. With a slotted spoon, carefully place egg in a bowl filled with ice water. Let cool completely for 5 minutes. Remove eggshell under cool running water. Let egg come to room temperature.

2. In work bowl fitted with metal blade, pulse egg, mayonnaise, chili sauce, olives, pickle, onion flakes, lemon juice, parsley, salt and black pepper until desired texture, about 10 times. For a chunky dressing, process for less time; for smooth, let the processor run for 1 minute. Refrigerate for at least 1 hour to allow the flavors to develop.

Blue Cheese Peppercorn Dressing

This rich and peppery dressing with a hint of blue cheese is a family favorite.

Tips

Dressing keeps, covered and refrigerated, for up to 2 weeks.

If all of the ingredients are at room temperature the dressing will be easier to blend.

Variation

If you would like a lower-fat dressing use low-fat cream cheese and sour cream. You will not sacrifice any flavor whatsoever.

4 oz	cream cheese, softened	125 g
4 oz	small curd cottage cheese	125 g
1/2 cup	sour cream	125 mL
1/4 cup	Traditional Mayonnaise (see recipe, page 36) or store-bought	50 mL
1/4 cup	buttermilk	50 mL
1 tbsp	freshly squeezed lemon juice	15 mL
1 1/2 tsp	loosely packed fresh dill	7 mL
1 1/2 tsp	dried onion flakes	7 mL
1 1/2 tsp	whole black peppercorns	7 mL
1/4 tsp	garlic powder	1 mL
2 oz	blue cheese, crumbled	60 g

1. In work bowl fitted with metal blade, process cream cheese, cottage cheese, sour cream, mayonnaise, buttermilk and lemon juice until smooth, about 2 minutes. Add dill, onion flakes, peppercorns and garlic powder. Process until well-blended, about 15 seconds.

2. Pour dressing into a medium bowl. Stir in blue cheese until blended. Let dressing stand, covered, in the refrigerator for a few hours to allow the flavors to develop.

Avocado Tamarind Cashew Dressing

I like serving this dressing over a cabbage salad.

Tips

Dressing keeps in an airtight container in the refrigerator for up to 2 weeks.

Tamarind can be found in the international section of most large grocery stores. Use the same amount of paste or seeded pulp if dried is not available.

Variation

Reduce the olive oil by half and use as a dipping sauce for Mini Chicken Puffs (see recipe, page 24).

¼ cup	unsalted roasted cashews	50 mL
⅔ cup	packed fresh cilantro leaves	150 mL
2	cloves garlic	2
2	green onions, green parts only, cut in half	2
½ cup	liquid honey	125 mL
1 tbsp	granulated sugar	15 mL
1 tbsp	white wine vinegar	15 mL
1 tsp	freshly ground black pepper	5 mL
1 tsp	ground cumin	5 mL
1 tsp	balsamic vinegar	5 mL
½ tsp	dried tamarind powder (see Tips, left)	2 mL
½ cup	extra virgin olive oil	125 mL
1	avocado	1

1. In work bowl fitted with metal blade, pulse cashews, cilantro, garlic and green onions until mixture is in small pieces, about 12 times.

2. In a microwave-safe container, combine honey, sugar, vinegar, black pepper, cumin, balsamic vinegar and tamarind. Microwave, uncovered, on High until steaming, about 45 seconds.

3. With the motor running, slowly pour honey mixture through the feed tube. Then drizzle olive oil through the feed tube until it has been incorporated into the dressing. Transfer to a covered container and refrigerate for at least 30 minutes to allow the flavors to develop.

4. Peel avocado, slice into small chunks and place in a bowl. Shake dressing and pour over avocado.

Raspberry Vinaigrette

*This dressing may seem
to be a lengthy process
but well worth the efforts
for the fresh flavor.*

Tips

Dressing keeps in bottle
or cruet in the refrigerator
for up to 3 weeks.

Make sure your berries
are free of blemishes and
soft spots.

Variation

Try blueberries or
strawberries in place of
the raspberries. Reduce
sugar if your berries
are sweet.

4 cups	loosely packed fresh raspberries	1 L
1 ¼ cups	white vinegar	300 mL
1 ½ cups	granulated sugar	375 mL
1 cup	vegetable oil	250 mL

1. Place raspberries in a jar and pour vinegar over top.
   Let stand in a cool dark place for 6 days, shaking once
   a day.

2. In work bowl fitted with metal blade, process raspberry
   mixture until smooth, about 2 minutes.

3. Strain mixture through a fine sieve into a saucepan over
   high heat. Add sugar and bring to a boil for 2 minutes.
   Let cool completely. Pour mixture back into work
   bowl fitted with metal blade. With the motor running,
   drizzle oil through the feed tube until it is incorporated.
   Pour dressing into a cruet or empty, cleaned salad
   dressing bottle.

Soups

Caramelized Onion and Mushroom Soup......52

Potato Leek Cheese Soup...................53

New England Clam Chowder................54

Chanterelle Oyster Bisque Soup.............55

Roasted Tomato Parmesan Soup.............56

Navy Bean Soup 58

Roasted Pecan Pumpkin Soup...............59

Hearty Cauliflower and Asparagus Soup.......60

French Onion Soup 62

Caramelized Onion and Mushroom Soup

Serves 6

On a cool fall evening this soup will warm your insides fast!

Tips

To store leftover soup, cool first to room temperature and place in an airtight container in the refrigerator for up to 4 days.

Using an array of different mushrooms deepens the flavor of this soup.

Variation

Try using 1 cup (250 mL) chopped leeks in place of the onion for a lighter flavor.

2 lbs	assorted mushrooms, such as button, chanterelles, morels or shiitake	1 kg
1/2	onion, quartered	1/2
3	cloves garlic	3
1/4 cup	unsalted butter	50 mL
1/4 cup	all-purpose flour	50 mL
1 cup	hot chicken stock	250 mL
6 cups	milk, at room temperature	1.5 L
1/2 tsp	salt	2 mL
1/2 tsp	ground white pepper	2 mL
1/4 cup	loosely packed Italian parsley	50 mL
2 tbsp	brandy	25 mL
1 cup	sour cream	250 mL

1. In work bowl fitted with slicing blade, slice mushrooms. Transfer to a bowl. Set aside.

2. Replace slicing blade with metal blade. Add onion and garlic and process until minced.

3. In a large saucepan over medium heat, melt butter. Add onion mixture and sauté until just starting to caramelize, 12 to 15 minutes. Add mushrooms and sauté until mushrooms are softened, 2 to 4 minutes. Sprinkle with flour and cook, stirring, for 3 minutes. Add chicken stock, stirring vigorously. Stir in milk, salt and white pepper. Bring to a simmer, stirring frequently to be sure the soup is not burning on the bottom of the pan, for 10 minutes. Add parsley and simmer for 10 minutes.

4. Stir in brandy and sour cream until heated through.

Potato Leek Cheese Soup

Serves 6

I like to serve this soup in a bread bowl made from the Honey Whole Wheat Sunflower Bread (see recipe, page 102).

Tips

To store leftover soup, cool first to room temperature and place in an airtight container in the refrigerator for up to 4 days.

To wash leeks: Cut the bulbs of the leeks in half. Fill sink with cold water and submerge, swishing them around to remove dirt.

If you forgot to warm cream prior to use, place in microwave for a few seconds and then use. If the cream is cold and you add it to the hot liquid it may curdle the soup.

Variation

If leeks are out of season or too expensive use 1 large diced sweet onion instead.

8 oz	Monterey Jack cheese, cut into chunks	250 g
2	russet potatoes, peeled and quartered (about 8 oz/250 g)	2
4	leeks, white and green parts only (see Tips, left)	4
1	onion, quartered	1
2	cloves garlic	2
2 tbsp	unsalted butter	25 mL
4 cups	chicken stock	1 L
1 cup	whipping (35%) cream, at room temperature (see Tips, left)	250 mL
¼ tsp	sea salt	1 mL
¼ tsp	ground white pepper	1 mL

1. In work bowl fitted with shredding blade, shred cheese. Transfer to a bowl. Set aside.

2. Replace shredding blade with slicing blade and slice potatoes. Transfer to another bowl. Set aside.

3. Replace slicing blade with metal blade. Add leeks, onion and garlic and process until finely chopped, about 30 seconds.

2. In a large saucepan over medium heat, melt butter. Add onion mixture and sauté until onion is opaque and leeks are wilted, 8 to 10 minutes. Add stock and bring to a gentle boil. Add cream and stir for a few minutes. Add reserved cheese and potatoes and cook until potatoes are fork tender, 15 to 20 minutes. Season with salt and white pepper.

New England Clam Chowder

Serves 8

I see so many mixes for clam chowder but it's so easy to make yourself. During the cold months I enjoy soup parties. You can serve this and a few other soups with the breads from Chapter 6.

Tips

To store leftover soup, cool first to room temperature and place in an airtight container in the refrigerator for up to 4 days.

If you can't find salt pork use the same amount of bacon instead.

Variation

Try adding 1½ cups (375 mL) chopped tomatoes (about 8 oz/250 g) and 2½ cups (625 mL) sliced mushrooms (about 8 oz/250 g) to the chowder.

6 oz	salt pork, cut into 4 chunks (see Tips, left)	175 g
1	large onion, quartered	1
3	stalks celery, cut in half	3
1	large leek, white and light green parts only (see Tips, page 53)	1
2 tbsp	all-purpose flour	25 mL
4 cups	hot water	1 L
¼ tsp	salt	1 mL
¼ tsp	ground white pepper	1 mL
⅛ tsp	ground nutmeg	0.5 mL
4 to 6	russet potatoes, peeled (about 1 lb/500 g)	4 to 6
5 cups	milk, at room temperature	1.25 L
1	can (16 oz/454 g) clams, drained	1

1. In work bowl fitted with metal blade, process pork and onion until minced, about 45 seconds. Transfer to a heavy-bottomed saucepan over medium heat. Sauté onion until softened, about 10 minutes. Skim the fat off the top.

2. Replace metal blade with slicing blade and slice celery and leek. Add to mixture in saucepan and sauté until soft, 12 to 15 minutes. Sprinkle with flour and cook, stirring to coat vegetables evenly, creating a golden roux, about 3 minutes. Gradually add hot water, stirring well to prevent lumps. Add salt, white pepper and nutmeg, stirring occasionally, until thickened, about 30 minutes.

3. Meanwhile, in same work bowl fitted with slicing blade, slice potatoes. Add to saucepan and simmer, stirring often, until potatoes are almost tender, for 15 minutes. Add milk and heat thoroughly, 10 to 12 minutes. Do not scorch or boil milk. Add clams and heat through. Taste and adjust seasonings.

Chanterelle Oyster Bisque Soup

Serves 6

The fresh taste of the chanterelle mushrooms and the flavorful oysters in this rich soup will warm you on a cool fall day.

Tips

To store leftover soup, cool first to room temperature and place in an airtight container in the refrigerator for up to 4 days.

Make sure your mushrooms are fresh. I like to purchase mine at my local farmer's market.

If chanterelle mushrooms are unavailable or too pricey, use button mushrooms instead.

½	shallot	½
I	stalk celery, cut in half	I
I lb	chanterelle mushrooms (see Tips, left)	500 g
2 tbsp	olive oil	25 mL
I tsp	dried oregano leaves	5 mL
I tsp	dried basil leaves	5 mL
I tsp	dried thyme leaves	5 mL
2 cups	chicken stock	500 mL
2 cups	whipping (35%) cream, at room temperature	500 mL
I	can (12 oz/375 g) chopped oysters, drained	I
Pinch	sea salt	Pinch
Pinch	ground white pepper	Pinch

1. In work bowl fitted with metal blade, process shallot and celery until finely chopped. Add mushrooms and pulse until coarsely chopped, 10 to 14 times.

2. Heat oil in a saucepan over medium heat. Add mushroom mixture and sauté until mushrooms are tender, 6 to 8 minutes. Add oregano, basil and thyme and sauté for 10 minutes. Add chicken stock and simmer for 3 minutes. Transfer, in batches, to work bowl fitted with metal blade and purée. Return to the saucepan. Stir in cream and oysters and heat through. Add salt and white pepper. Serve hot.

Roasted Tomato Parmesan Soup

The fresh flavors of ripe tomatoes and rich Parmesan cheese will make you feel as though you are in the hills of Tuscany.

Tips

To store leftover soup, cool first to room temperature and place in an airtight container in the refrigerator for up to 4 days.

Make sure the tomatoes are fully blistered and steamed so you can remove the skins easily.

Variation

Try using heirloom tomatoes for a different look and taste.

- *Preheat broiler*
- *Baking sheet, lined with parchment paper*

6 oz	Parmesan cheese, cut into chunks	175 g
½ cup	loosely packed fresh basil leaves	125 mL
1½ lbs	Roma tomatoes (10 to 14 tomatoes)	750 g
2 tbsp	unsalted butter	25 mL
2 tbsp	all-purpose flour	25 mL
2 cups	milk, at room temperature, divided	500 mL
2 cups	whipping (35%) cream, at room temperature	500 mL
¼ tsp	ground white pepper	1 mL
Pinch	salt	Pinch

1. In work bowl fitted with metal blade, with the motor running, add Parmesan cheese through the feed tube and process until finely grated. Transfer to a small bowl. Set aside.

2. In same work bowl fitted with metal blade, pulse basil leaves until finally chopped, 8 to 10 times. Transfer to another bowl. Set aside.

3. Cut tomatoes in half crosswise and core. Squeeze seeds and membranes out. Place on prepared baking sheet, skin side up. Broil in preheated oven until skins blister, about 10 minutes. Transfer to a plastic bag and let stand to steam, about 10 minutes. Peel off charred skins and discard. Set tomatoes aside.

4. In a large saucepan over medium heat, melt butter. Add flour and cook, stirring, until a thick paste forms but does not brown. Whisk in $\frac{1}{4}$ cup (50 mL) of the milk and cook, whisking constantly, until thickened, about 3 minutes. Whisk in remaining milk and cream. Add tomatoes, basil and half of the Parmesan cheese and heat through. Season with white pepper and salt. Ladle into soup bowls and garnish each bowl with remaining cheese.

Navy Bean Soup

When I was young I remember Mom making this flavorful soup after Christmas so she could use the leftover ham.

Tips

To store leftover soup, cool first to room temperature and place in an airtight container in the refrigerator for up to 4 days.

You can soak the beans the night before to speed up the process and omit cooking in Step 1.

Variation

I like to take half of the cooked beans and purée them with the metal blade and then add them back to the stew to create a richer-tasting stock.

1 lb	dry navy (white pea) beans (about 2 cups/500 mL)	500 g
3	large carrots, cut into 3-inch (7.5 cm) lengths	3
2	stalks celery, cut into 3-inch (7.5 cm) lengths	2
1	large onion, quartered	1
6 cups	water	1.5 L
8 oz	sliced ham or bacon	250 g
2 tbsp	granulated sugar (approx.)	25 mL
1 tsp	salt	5 mL
1 tsp	ground white pepper	5 mL

1. Wash beans in a colander and sort, discarding stones and blemished beans. Place beans in a large saucepan and cover with cold water by 1 inch (2.5 cm). Bring to a boil over high heat. Boil for 2 minutes. Remove from heat, cover and let stand for 1 hour. Drain and return to saucepan.

2. In work bowl fitted with slicing blade, slice carrots, celery and onion.

3. Add carrot mixture to beans with 6 cups (1.5 L) water and bring to a simmer over high heat.

4. Replace slicing blade with metal blade. Add ham and pulse until chopped, about 10 times. Add to saucepan. Reduce heat and simmer, covered, stirring occasionally, until beans are very tender, about $1\frac{1}{2}$ hours. Add sugar, to taste, salt and white pepper.

Roasted Pecan Pumpkin Soup

Serves 8

One fall when I had too much fresh pumpkin left over and was tired of making pies, I decided to create this creamy and nutty soup.

Tips

To store leftover soup, cool first to room temperature and place in an airtight container in the refrigerator for up to 4 days.

If cream is not at room temperature it may curdle when you add it to the soup.

Variation

I like to use pine nuts in place of pecans but I don't process them. I like to keep them whole.

I	onion, quartered	I
½ cup	pecan halves	125 mL
I	clove garlic	I
6 cups	chicken stock	1.5 L
2¼ cups	Pumpkin Purée (see recipe, page 86) or canned pumpkin purée (not pie filling)	550 mL
1½ tsp	salt	7 mL
½ tsp	dried thyme leaves	2 mL
½ tsp	ground white pepper	2 mL
½ cup	whipping (35%) cream, at room temperature	125 mL
8	parsley sprigs	8

1. In work bowl fitted with metal blade, process onion, pecans and garlic until finely chopped.

2. Transfer mixture to a large saucepan over medium heat and sauté until onions are opaque and pecans are light brown, 5 to 8 minutes. Add chicken stock, pumpkin purée, salt, thyme and white pepper. Bring to a simmer. Reduce heat to low and simmer, uncovered, for 20 minutes. Stir in cream. Garnish with parsley sprigs.

Hearty Cauliflower and Asparagus Soup

Your guests will think you laced this soup with cream because of the rich flavor, but it all comes from the vegetables.

Tips

To store leftover soup, cool first to room temperature and place in an airtight container in the refrigerator for up to 4 days.

If the soup seems a little thick, add additional stock or wine.

Variation

For an all-green soup for St. Patrick's Day substitute broccoli for the cauliflower.

1	onion, quartered	1
2 tbsp	unsalted butter	25 mL
6	cloves garlic, minced	6
2½ cups	cauliflower florets	625 mL
2 tbsp	dry white wine	25 mL
1	large bunch asparagus (about 1 lb/500 g), divided	1
3 cups	chicken stock, divided	750 mL
2 tbsp	all-purpose flour	25 mL
1 tsp	salt	5 mL
½ tsp	ground white pepper	2 mL
Pinch	ground nutmeg	Pinch
¼ cup	loosely packed fresh basil leaves	50 mL

1. In work bowl fitted with slicing blade, slice onion.

2. In a large saucepan over medium heat, melt butter. Add onion and garlic and sauté until onion is opaque, 5 to 7 minutes. Add cauliflower and wine. Cook for 2 minutes. Reduce heat to low and simmer while continuing with the recipe.

3. Replace slicing blade with metal blade. Add half of the asparagus and purée until smooth. If it seems a bit dry, add a few tablespoons (25 mL) of the chicken stock through the feed tube. Transfer to saucepan.

4. Trim ¼ inch (0.5 cm) from the ends of remaining asparagus. Discard ends. Slice stems on a diagonal into ¼- to ½-inch (0.5 to 1 cm) pieces. Add to saucepan.

5. Pour 2 cups (500 mL) of the stock into the pot and bring to a simmer. Meanwhile, pour ½ cup (125 mL) of the stock into a small bowl. Add flour, salt, white pepper and nutmeg and whisk until smooth. Add to the saucepan and cook, stirring, until thickened, 3 to 5 minutes. Add remaining stock.

6. In same work bowl fitted with metal blade, add basil and pulse just until chopped slightly, about 5 times. Stir into soup.

French Onion Soup

Serves 6

This is a simple soup to make, yet it always seems to cost a great deal in a restaurant.

Tips

To store leftover soup, after Step 3 cool first to room temperature and place in an airtight container in the refrigerator for up to 4 days. Reheat until steaming before proceeding with Step 4.

You can use a torch similar to one used for crème brûlée instead of the broiler to brown the cheese.

Variation

To make soup spicier, add 1 tsp (5 mL) hot pepper sauce just before serving.

12 oz	Monterey Jack cheese, cut into chunks	375 g
3	large sweet onions, quartered	3
1/4 cup	unsalted butter	50 mL
2 tbsp	granulated sugar	25 mL
1 tbsp	all-purpose flour	15 mL
2 2/3 cups	beef stock, divided	650 mL
2 cups	warm water	500 mL
1 tsp	Worcestershire sauce	5 mL
3	drops hot pepper sauce	3
6	slices baguette, toasted	6

1. In work bowl fitted with shredding blade, shred cheese. Transfer to a bowl. Set aside.

2. Replace shredding blade with slicing blade and slice onions. Transfer to another bowl. Set aside.

3. In a saucepan over medium heat, sauté butter and sugar until melted, about 3 minutes. Add onions and cook, stirring occasionally, until tender and just beginning to brown and caramelize, 12 to 18 minutes. Stir in flour. Gradually stir in half of the stock. Bring to a boil, stirring constantly. Stir in remaining stock, water, Worcestershire sauce and hot pepper sauce and bring to a gentle boil. Boil gently for 12 minutes. Reduce heat to low and simmer for 5 minutes. Meanwhile, preheat broiler.

4. Place 1 slice baguette in each of 6 heatproof bowls and pour soup over top. Sprinkle with cheese. Place bowls under preheated broiler until cheese is melted and light brown, 4 to 5 minutes. Serve immediately.

Main Courses

Macadamia-Crusted Salmon 64

Cold Shrimp Salad. 65

Seafood Pâté 66

Three Herb-Crusted Scallops 68

New Orleans Bourbon Chicken 69

Jerk Chicken. 70

Mushroom-Crusted Chicken 72

Potato Chip Chicken. 73

Turkey Meatballs 74

Stuffed Chicken Breasts 75

Chicken Rockefeller. 76

Fast and Easy Meat Loaf. 77

Red Hot Chili. 78

Mushroom-Stuffed Pork Chops. 79

Tuscan Pork Chops 80

Baked Beef Burgundy 81

Jamaican Seafood Rub 82

Hot and Spicy BBQ Rub 83

Drunken Fresh Herb Marinade. 84

Macadamia-Crusted Salmon

Serves 6

Macadamia nuts are one of the hardest and oiliest nuts, but so flavorful. Here they make a great rub for salmon. Serve with Raspberry Sauce (see recipe, page 180), if desired.

Tip

If you only can locate salted macadamia nuts, rub them in paper towels to remove as much salt as possible.

Variation

You can use whitefish in place of the salmon. Adjust cooking time depending upon thickness.

- *Preheat broiler*
- *Large baking pan, lined with parchment paper*

½ cup	unsalted macadamia nuts (see Tips, left)	125 mL
1 cup	broken pieces stone-ground wheat crackers	250 mL
2 tbsp	all-purpose flour	25 mL
1 tsp	fresh dill	5 mL
3 tbsp	olive oil	45 mL
4	salmon fillets (about 1½ lbs/750 g)	4

1. In work bowl fitted with metal blade, combine macadamia nuts, crackers, flour and dill. Process until finely ground. Place in a shallow dish.

2. Rub oil on both sides of fillets. Dredge fillets in nut mixture. Discard any extra mixture.

3. In prepared baking pan, place fillets skin-side up, at least 2 inches (5 cm) apart. Broil under preheated broiler, turning once, until surface of fish springs back when lightly pressed, 2 to 3 minutes per side.

Hearty Cauliflower and Asparagus Soup (page 60)

Overleaf: Ribs with Hot and Spicy BBQ Rub (page 83)

Cold Shrimp Salad

Here's a refreshing light meal that doesn't require an oven. Perfect for those hot summer months.

Tip

I love serving this salad with Whole Wheat Rolls (see recipe, page 112).

Variation

Try using cooked scallops in place of the shrimp.

2	sweet pickles, cut in half (about 2 oz/60 g)	2
1 lb	cooked salad shrimp	500 g
½ cup	Traditional Mayonnaise (see recipe, page 36) or store-bought	125 mL
1 tbsp	loosely packed fresh dill	15 mL
1 tsp	prepared mustard	5 mL
4 cups	salad greens	1 L
4	tomatoes (about 12 oz/375 g)	4
1	avocado, peeled and pitted	1
½ cup	Avocado Tamarind Cashew Dressing (see recipe, page 49)	125 mL

1. In work bowl fitted with metal blade, add pickles and pulse until finely chopped, about 10 times. Add shrimp, mayonnaise, dill and mustard and pulse until coarsely chopped, about 10 times. Transfer to a small bowl.

2. Divide salad greens evenly among 4 plates. Cut tomatoes and avocado into wedges. Fan over salad greens. Scoop about one-quarter of the shrimp mixture over each salad. Drizzle 2 tbsp (25 mL) of the Avocado Tamarind Cashew Dressing over top.

Chicken Rockefeller (page 76)

Seafood Pâté

Serves 8

I like to serve this pâté cold on a bed of greens drizzled with a light vinaigrette for a summer brunch.

Tips

Pâté keeps well, wrapped in plastic wrap and refrigerated, for up to 2 days.

Purchase shrimp on sale. I use the cooked salad shrimp because it will be chopped up anyway.

Variation

Try scallops in place of shrimp if you find a bargain at the market.

- *Preheat oven to 325°F (160°C)*
- *Place a large pan filled with hot water on the lower rack*
- *11-by 7-inch (2 L) baking dish, lined with plastic wrap*

1	bunch fresh spinach (about 12 oz/375 g)	1
1	bunch fresh Italian parsley (about 6 oz/175 g)	1
4	green onions, cut in half	4
2 tsp	unsalted butter	10 mL
6 oz	whitefish	175 g
1	egg white	1
2 tbsp	whipping (35%) cream	25 mL
8 oz	shrimp, shelled and cut into small pieces (see Tips, left)	250 g
2 tsp	chopped fresh tarragon	10 mL
1/8 tsp	ground white pepper	0.5 mL
1/8 tsp	freshly ground nutmeg	0.5 mL

1. Discard stems from spinach and parsley. Wash leaves and place in a salad spinner to dry.

2. In work bowl fitted with metal blade, pulse spinach, parsley and green onions until coarsely chopped, about 10 times.

3. In a skillet over medium heat, melt butter. Add spinach mixture and sauté until greens start to wilt, about 3 minutes. Transfer to a bowl and refrigerate until cold, about 30 minutes.

4. In same work bowl fitted with metal blade, add whitefish and purée for 30 seconds. Add egg white and process for 30 seconds. With the motor running, add cream through the feed tube. Add to bowl with spinach mixture and combine. Add shrimp, tarragon, white pepper and nutmeg.

5. Scoop into prepared baking dish, smoothing top. Cover with foil. Place in preheated oven on rack above pan of water and bake until set, about 25 minutes. Let stand to firm up completely and cool. Remove from pan and remove foil. Slice with a sharp knife. Serve.

Three Herb-Crusted Scallops

Fresh herbs make the flavor in these scallops pop. Serve with Roasted Red Pepper Velvet Sauce (see recipe, page 178), if desired.

Tip

Make sure you purchase sea scallops because bay scallops are smaller and less flavorful.

Variation

To add more spice to the scallops, add 1 tsp (5 mL) hot pepper sauce to the herb mixture.

2 cups	broken pieces stone-ground wheat crackers	500 mL
2 tbsp	all-purpose flour	25 mL
1 tsp	fresh tarragon leaves	5 mL
1 tsp	fresh rosemary leaves	5 mL
1 tsp	loosely packed fresh dill	5 mL
12 oz	sea scallops (about 16)	375 g
3 tbsp	olive oil	45 mL
1 tbsp	unsalted butter	15 mL

1. In work bowl fitted with metal blade, process crackers, flour, tarragon, rosemary and dill until finely ground. Transfer to a shallow dish.

2. Rub oil on both sides of scallops. Dredge scallops in herb mixture. Discard any extra mixture.

3. In a large skillet over medium heat, melt butter. Add scallops, in batches to prevent crowding, and cook, turning once, until light brown and surface springs back when lightly pressed, about 4 minutes per side.

New Orleans Bourbon Chicken

The French quarter of New Orleans is filled with great restaurants. Here's a dish that's served in a few of the older establishments.

Tip

To peel fresh ginger, use a large spoon and scrape off the outer peeling.

Variation

You can also use this to make flavorful wings. Just substitute 2 lbs (1 kg) wings for the chicken breasts and serve as an appetizer.

- *Preheat oven to 400°F (200°C)*
- *13-by 9-inch (3 L) shallow baking dish, buttered*

6	skinless boneless chicken breasts (about 2 lbs/1 kg)	6
8	cloves garlic	8
1	piece (about 1½ inches/4 cm long) fresh ginger, peeled and cut into 3 chunks	1
6	green onions, cut in half	6
1	small onion, quartered	1
1 cup	low-sodium soy sauce (see Tip, page 94)	250 mL
½ cup	lightly packed brown sugar	125 mL
½ cup	bourbon	125 mL
¼ cup	olive oil	50 mL

1. In prepared baking dish, place chicken breasts in a single layer. Set aside.

2. In work bowl fitted with metal blade, pulse garlic, ginger, green onions and onion until coarsely chopped, about 20 times. With the motor running, add soy sauce, brown sugar and bourbon through the feed tube. Drizzle olive oil through the feed tube until incorporated. Pour mixture over chicken breasts and turn to coat underside.

3. Bake in preheated oven until chicken is no longer pink inside, 20 to 25 minutes. Spoon some of the sauce over cooked chicken for presentation.

Jerk Chicken

Serves 4

Jerk is a Caribbean spice mixture that is very popular in Jamaica and is used most often as a rub or marinade for chicken or pork. You can vary the intensity of the heat by increasing or decreasing the marinating time (see Tip, below).

Tip

If you like just a little kick, marinate the chicken for only 10 minutes. For the full effect, marinate for the entire 45 minutes.

Variation

If you don't want so much heat, reduce the chiles to 3.

- *Preheat oven to 375°F (190°C)*
- *Roasting pan, greased*
- *Instant-read thermometer*

1	roasting chicken (about 3 to 4 lbs/1.5 to 2 kg), cut into pieces	1
2 tbsp	olive oil	25 mL
6	green onions, white and green parts only, cut in half	6
5	cloves garlic	5
1	onion, quartered	1
6	habanero chiles, stemmed, seeded and cut in half	6
2 tbsp	lightly packed brown sugar	25 mL
1½ tbsp	sea salt	22 mL
1 tbsp	loosely packed fresh thyme leaves	15 mL
2 tsp	ground allspice	10 mL
2 tsp	whole black peppercorns	10 mL
¾ tsp	freshly ground nutmeg	4 mL
½ tsp	ground cinnamon	2 mL
¼ tsp	ground ginger	1 mL
¼ cup	freshly squeezed lime juice	50 mL
¼ cup	olive oil	50 mL
3 tbsp	low-sodium soy sauce (see Tip, page 94)	45 mL

1. In prepared roasting pan, coat chicken parts with oil. Arrange in a single layer. Set aside.

2. In work bowl fitted with metal blade, process green onions, garlic, onion and chiles until finely chopped, about 2 minutes. Add brown sugar, sea salt, thyme, allspice, peppercorns, nutmeg, cinnamon and ginger and pulse until blended, about 10 times. With the motor running, add lime juice, olive oil and soy sauce through the feed tube until incorporated.

3. Pour mixture over chicken pieces. Let marinate in the refrigerator for 45 minutes (see Tips, page 70). Bake in preheated oven, uncovered, until juices run clear when chicken is pierced and an instant-read thermometer inserted into the thickest part of the thigh registers 175°F (80°C), 40 to 45 minutes.

Mushroom-Crusted Chicken

This recipe is adapted from one by Kathie Alex, who conducts food tours in the south of France in the former home of Julia Child. I visit yearly on a culinary tour with students.

Tip

To make an even layer of mushroom filling, I press the filling first on plastic wrap and then transfer it to the chicken.

Variation

You can use the same amount of fresh herbs, such as dill or tarragon, in place of the herbes de Provence.

- *Preheat oven to 400°F (200°C)*
- *13-by 9-inch (3 L) shallow baking dish, lined with parchment paper*

6	skinless boneless chicken breasts (about 2 lbs/1 kg)	6
2 tbsp	olive oil	25 mL
8 oz	button mushrooms, stems removed	250 g
2 tbsp	Dijon mustard	25 mL
1 tbsp	herbes de Provence	15 mL
2 tsp	freshly ground black pepper	10 mL
1 tsp	salt	5 mL

1. In a shallow baking dish, coat chicken with olive oil. Arrange in a single layer. Set aside.

2. In work bowl fitted with metal blade, add mushrooms and pulse until smooth with a few large pieces left. Transfer to a bowl. Add mustard, herbes de Provence, black pepper and salt until well combined.

3. Press a thin layer of mushroom filling over top of each chicken breast (see Tip, left).

4. Bake in preheated oven until chicken is no longer pink inside, 20 to 25 minutes.

Potato Chip Chicken

I loved the crunchy texture of this chicken, which my Mom would make when I was young.

Tip

Make sure the potato chips are fresh. If they are stale you can crisp them up in a preheated 400°F (200°C) oven for 5 minutes before processing.

Variation

Use flavored potato chips, such as barbecue.

• *Preheat oven to 400°F (200°C)*
• *13-by 9-inch (3 L) shallow baking dish, lined with parchment paper*

1	bag (2 oz/60 g) potato chips (about 2 cups/500 mL)	1
2	cloves garlic	2
1 tsp	paprika	5 mL
2 tbsp	olive oil	25 mL
6	skinless boneless chicken breasts (about 2 lbs/1 kg)	6

1. In work bowl fitted with metal blade, process potato chips, garlic and paprika until finely ground, about 30 seconds. Transfer to a shallow dish.

2. Rub oil over chicken breasts. Dredge breasts in potato chip mixture. Arrange in a single layer in prepared baking dish. Discard any extra mixture.

3. Bake in preheated oven until chicken is no longer pink inside, 20 to 25 minutes.

Turkey Meatballs

Serves 6

Keep a batch of these meatballs in the freezer for a fast dinner.

Tip
To freeze, cool completely, place in resealable plastic freezer bags and freeze for up to 3 months. Thaw in the refrigerator overnight and microwave until hot, 12 to 18 minutes.

Variations

You can substitute ground beef for the turkey.

- Preheat oven to 350°F (180°C)
- 13-by 9-inch (3 L) baking dish

1 cup	Fresh Bread Crumbs (see recipe, page 26)	250 mL
1 cup	milk	250 mL
1	onion, quartered	1
2 lbs	ground turkey	1 kg
2	eggs	2
½ tsp	ground ginger	2 mL
½ tsp	salt	2 mL
½ tsp	freshly ground black pepper	2 mL
¼ tsp	freshly ground nutmeg	1 mL
2 tbsp	vegetable oil	25 mL

1. In a large bowl, combine bread crumbs with milk until absorbed.

2. In work bowl fitted with metal blade, add onion and pulse 10 times. Transfer to bowl with bread crumbs.

3. In same work bowl fitted with metal blade, process ground turkey, eggs, ginger, salt, black pepper and nutmeg until blended, about 2 minutes. Add to bread crumb mixture and blend together well. Shape mixture into 36 balls, each about 2 inches (5 cm).

4. Heat oil in a large skillet over medium heat. Sauté meatballs, turning often, until light brown on all sides, about 6 minutes. Place in baking dish and cover with foil. Bake in preheated oven until no longer pink inside, 20 to 25 minutes. Drain off any excess oil. Serve hot.

Stuffed Chicken Breasts

Serves 6

I started looking in the refrigerator for leftovers and created this flavorful chicken dish.

Tips

If the ham is very salty, omit the salt in the recipe.

To toast pine nuts: Place nuts in a dry skillet over medium heat and cook, stirring, until they begin to brown, 3 to 4 minutes.

Variation

Use gorgonzola or blue cheese in place of the feta.

- *Preheat oven to 400°F (200°C)*
- *13-by 9-inch (3 L) baking dish, buttered*

6	skinless boneless chicken breasts (about 2 lbs/1 kg)	6
2 tbsp	olive oil	25 mL
FILLING		
3 oz	feta cheese, crumbled	90 g
3 oz	salami or cured ham	90 g
2 tsp	loosely packed fresh tarragon leaves	10 mL
1/4 cup	toasted pine nuts (see Tips, left)	50 mL
1/2 tsp	ground white pepper	2 mL
1/4 tsp	onion powder	1 mL
1/4 tsp	salt	1 mL

1. Slice a 2-inch (5 cm) slit horizontally into each chicken breast to form a pocket. Rub chicken breasts with olive oil. Set aside.

2. *Filling:* In work bowl fitted with metal blade, process feta cheese, salami and tarragon until smooth, about 3 minutes. Transfer to a bowl. Fold in pine nuts, white pepper, onion powder and salt.

3. Fill pockets of chicken breasts with cheese mixture. Arrange in prepared baking dish in a single layer. Bake in preheated oven until chicken is no longer pink inside, 25 to 30 minutes.

Chicken Rockefeller

Serves 4

*I took the famous 1890s'
recipe for oysters
Rockefeller originally
made in New Orleans
and named after John
D. Rockefeller (because
it was so rich) and
created this dish with
chicken.*

Tips

Cover any leftovers
and refrigerate for up
to 4 days. Reheat in a
preheated 350°F (180°C)
oven until hot in the
center, 18 to 20 minutes.

If you have frozen
spinach, just thaw and
drain a 12 oz (375 g)
package and use like
the fresh.

Variation

Try the same amount of
fresh basil leaves in place
of the spinach.

- *Preheat oven to 400°F (200°C)*
- *13-by 9-inch (3 L) baking dish, buttered*

4	skinless boneless chicken breasts (about 1½ lbs/750 g)	4
2 tsp	olive oil	10 mL
½ cup	Fresh Bread Crumbs (see recipe, page 26)	125 mL
4 oz	provolone cheese, cut into chunks	125 g
1	bunch fresh spinach, trimmed (about 12 oz/375 g)	1
1	onion, quartered	1
2 tsp	unsalted butter, melted	10 mL
1 tsp	anise-flavored liqueur, such as Pernod	5 mL
¼ cup	loosely packed fresh parsley sprigs	50 mL

1. Coat both sides of chicken breasts with olive oil and dredge in bread crumbs. Arrange in a prepared baking dish in a single layer. Set aside. Discard any excess crumbs.

2. In work bowl fitted with shredding blade, shred provolone cheese. Transfer to a small bowl.

3. Replace shredding blade with metal blade and pulse spinach and onion until finely chopped, about 20 times. Transfer to another bowl. Stir in butter and liqueur until combined.

4. Spoon one-quarter of the mixture over each chicken breast. Top with grated cheese and parsley sprigs.

5. Bake in preheated oven until chicken is no longer pink inside, about 20 minutes. Transfer chicken to serving plates and spoon remaining sauce over top.

Fast and Easy Meat Loaf

Serves 6

I love fast and easy dishes that you can prepare days in advance of needing them. This one fits the bill.

Tips

Cooked meat loaf keeps, covered and refrigerated, for up to 2 days. To reheat, place in a preheated 400°F (200°C) oven until warm inside, 10 to 15 minutes for slices.

Make sure the beef broth is hot because it will incorporate more easily.

Variation

You can substitute all ground turkey for the beef and sausage if you like.

- *Preheat oven to 325°F (160°C)*
- *9-by 5-inch (2 L) loaf pan, lined with parchment paper*
- *Instant-read thermometer*

1 lb	ground beef	500 g
1 lb	ground mild sausage (casings removed)	500 g
3	eggs	3
2 cups	Fresh Bread Crumbs (see recipe, page 26)	500 mL
1	onion, quartered	1
1/2	red bell pepper, cut into large pieces	1/2
1/2	yellow bell pepper, cut into large pieces	1/2
2	cloves garlic	2
1	can (6 oz/175 g) tomato paste (about 3/4 cup/175 mL)	1
1/2 cup	hot beef stock (see Tips, left)	125 mL
1 1/2 tsp	onion powder	7 mL
1 tsp	paprika	5 mL
1/8 tsp	salt	0.5 mL
1/8 tsp	freshly ground black pepper	0.5 mL

1. In a large bowl, combine ground beef, sausage, eggs and bread crumbs. Set aside.

2. In work bowl fitted with metal blade, pulse onion, red and yellow peppers and garlic until chunky, about 20 times. Transfer to bowl with meat mixture. Add tomato paste, beef stock, onion powder, paprika, salt and black pepper. Mix well.

3. Transfer to prepared loaf pan, packing firmly. Bake in preheated oven for 30 minutes. Then increase temperature to 375°F (190°C) and bake until firm when pressed on top and an instant-read thermometer inserted in the center of the loaf registers 160°F (71°C), about 45 minutes. Let loaf rest for at least 20 minutes before removing from the pan and slicing.

Red Hot Chili

This is a crowd-pleasing recipe for a tailgate party. You can save the leftovers but I warn you: the chili gets hotter every day!

Tip

Make sure you wear plastic gloves when handling the hot peppers because the hot seeds and oil will stay on your skin and burn your eyes if you rub them.

Variation

For a hotter chili, add additional jalapeño peppers to your heat threshold.

1	large onion, quartered	1
1	green bell pepper, quartered	1
2	stalks celery, cut into 3-inch (7.5 cm) pieces	2
2	jalapeño peppers, cut in half and seeded	2
4	cloves garlic	4
2 tbsp	vegetable oil	25 mL
4 lbs	lean ground beef	2 kg
1	can (6 oz/175 mL) tomato paste (about ¾ cup/175 mL)	1
1	can (28 oz/796 mL) stewed tomatoes, including juice, coarsely chopped	1
1 tbsp	chili powder	15 mL
1 tbsp	sea salt	15 mL
1 tbsp	freshly ground black pepper	15 mL
½ tsp	dried oregano leaves	2 mL
½ tsp	garlic salt	2 mL

1. In work bowl fitted with metal blade, pulse onion, green pepper, celery, jalapeño and garlic until finely chopped, about 15 times.

2. Heat oil in a large saucepan over medium heat. Add onion mixture and sauté until onions are opaque, about 10 minutes. Add ground beef and cook, stirring and breaking up beef, until no longer pink, 10 to 15 minutes. Stir in tomato paste and stewed tomatoes with juice. Add chili powder, sea salt, black pepper, oregano and garlic salt and simmer for 30 minutes. Taste and adjust salt and pepper. Let simmer for 2½ hours, stirring every 10 to 15 minutes.

Mushroom-Stuffed Pork Chops

Here's the perfect way to serve pork chops, with the vegetable cooked right in!

Tip

If the filling starts to leak during cooking, you can always spoon it over the cooked chops when serving.

Variation

Try provolone cheese in place of the Swiss.

6	bone-in pork chops, about 1 1/2 inches (4 cm) thick	6
2 tsp	olive oil	10 mL
Pinch	salt	Pinch
1/2 cup	button mushrooms, cleaned and stemmed	125 mL
3 oz	Swiss cheese, cut into chunks	90 g
3	green onions, cut into 3-inch (7.5 cm) lengths	3
4	drops hot pepper sauce	4
1 tsp	unsalted butter, divided	5 mL

1. With a sharp knife, cut a slit horizontally to make a pocket in side of each pork chop opposite bone, working almost but not quite to edges. Rub outside of chops with olive oil and sprinkle with salt.

2. In work bowl fitted with metal blade, pulse mushrooms, cheese, green onions and hot pepper sauce until in small pieces, about 15 times. Fill chops with mushroom mixture, trying not to overstuff the pockets.

3. In a large skillet over medium heat, melt 1/2 tsp (2 mL) of the butter. Add chops, in batches as necessary to prevent crowding, and cook, turning once, until pork is slightly pink inside, about 8 minutes per side. Add remaining butter in between batches as necessary to prevent sticking.

Tuscan Pork Chops

Direct from the rolling hills of Tuscany! Try these all-Italian pork chops.

Tip

Try frying capers some time for another use. They pop like popcorn and taste great in a salad.

Variation

You can serve this with canned spaghetti sauce over top for an added touch.

4 oz	Parmesan cheese, cut into chunks	125 g
1 tbsp	drained capers	15 mL
2 tsp	dried oregano leaves	10 mL
½ tsp	garlic powder	2 mL
6	bone-in pork chops, about 1 inch (2.5 cm) thick	6
2 tsp	olive oil	10 mL
2 tbsp	unsalted butter, divided	25 mL

1. In work bowl fitted with metal blade, with the motor running, add Parmesan cheese through the feed tube and process until grated. Transfer to a shallow dish.

2. In same work bowl fitted with metal blade, process capers, oregano and garlic powder until a paste-like consistency, about 30 seconds. Transfer to dish with cheese and combine.

3. Rub both sides of pork chops with olive oil. Dredge pork chops in cheese mixture. Discard any excess mixture.

4. In a large skillet over medium heat, melt 1 tbsp (15 mL) butter. Add chops, in batches as necessary to prevent crowding, and cook, turning once, until pork is slightly pink inside, 3 to 4 minutes per side. Add remaining butter in between batches as necessary to prevent sticking.

Baked Beef Burgundy

The flavorful taste of burgundy wine in this dish will warm you up during the cold winter months.

Tip

Always use a good-quality Burgundy or merlot wine that's good enough to drink.

Variation

Try using pork cubes in place of the beef.

● *Preheat oven to 325°F (160°C)*

5	large carrots, cut into 3-inch (7.5 cm) lengths (about 12 oz/375 g)	5
6	stalks celery, cut into 3-inch (7.5 cm) lengths	6
3	large onions, quartered (about 1 lb/500 g)	3
12 oz	button mushrooms, stemmed	375 g
¼ cup	all-purpose flour	50 mL
¼ cup	low-sodium soy sauce (see Tip, page 94)	50 mL
4	cloves garlic	4
3 lbs	stewing beef, cut into 3- to 3½-inch (7.5 to 8.5 cm) cubes	1.5 kg
1½ cups	Burgundy wine (see Tip, left)	375 mL
½ tsp	freshly ground black pepper	2 mL
½ tsp	dried thyme leaves	2 mL
	Cooked rice or noodles	

1. In work bowl fitted with slicing blade, slice carrots, celery and onions, in batches if necessary. Transfer to a large ovenproof saucepan.

2. In same work bowl fitted with slicing blade, slice mushrooms. Transfer to a bowl.

3. Replace slicing blade with metal blade and add flour. With the motor running, pour soy sauce though the feed tube. Add garlic and process until smooth. Transfer to saucepan with carrot mixture. Add beef, wine, black pepper and thyme.

4. Bake, covered tightly, in preheated oven for 1 hour. Add reserved mushrooms. Bake until beef is fork tender, about 1 hour more. Serve over rice or noodles.

Jamaican Seafood Rub

I love the islands and the spicy foods that are often served. Here's a rub for scallops and shrimp. Make sure you have rum punch close by.

Tip

To roast sunflower seeds: Place seeds on a baking sheet and roast in a preheated 400°F (200°C) oven for 10 minutes.

Variation

You can deep-fry the scallops or shrimp in a deep fryer for a crunchy texture.

¼ cup	unsalted sunflower seeds, roasted (see Tip, left)	50 mL
2 tbsp	ground turmeric	25 mL
2 tbsp	cumin seeds	25 mL
1 tbsp	coriander seeds	15 mL
1 tbsp	ground cinnamon	15 mL
1 tbsp	ground ginger	15 mL
1½ tsp	mustard seeds	7 mL
1½ tsp	whole cloves	7 mL
1½ tsp	hot pepper flakes	7 mL
1 tsp	celery seeds	5 mL
1½ lbs	sea scallops, or 18 jumbo shrimp, peeled and deveined	750 g
¼ cup	vegetable oil	50 mL

1. In work bowl fitted with metal blade, process sunflower seeds, turmeric, cumin and coriander seeds, cinnamon, ginger, mustard seeds, whole cloves, hot pepper flakes and celery seeds until powdery, about 2 minutes. Before opening the food processor and transferring to a shallow dish, allow the mixture to settle for a few seconds. Otherwise, it will fly all over the place. Rub can be refrigerated in an airtight container for up to 6 months.

2. *To use:* Place ¼ cup (50 mL) of the rub in a shallow dish. In batches, add seafood and press to coat in rub, shaking off excess. Discard any excess rub from dish.

3. Heat oil in a large skillet over medium heat. Add seafood and sauté, turning once, until firm to the touch, about 2 minutes per side. If the scallops or shrimp are large, you may have to sauté another 2 minutes. Serve warm.

Hot and Spicy BBQ Rub

I can never go to Memphis, Tennessee, without having ribs! This city is known for their dry rub ribs. Here is a similar rub for you to try.

Tips

Rub keeps stored in an airtight container for up to 6 months.

If the mixture becomes hard and dry, just place in the microwave on Low for 3 minutes and stir.

Variation

Add 2 cups (500 mL) Homemade Ketchup (see recipe, page 176) or store-bought to make this rub a wet sauce.

1 cup	lightly packed brown sugar	250 mL
2/3 cup	chili powder	150 mL
1/4 cup	paprika	50 mL
2 tbsp	garlic salt	25 mL
2 tbsp	coarse sea salt	25 mL
1 tbsp	whole black peppercorns	15 mL
2 tsp	mustard seeds	10 mL
2 tsp	granulated sugar	10 mL
1 tsp	ground ginger	5 mL
1 tsp	whole cloves	5 mL
1/4 tsp	ground turmeric	1 mL
1/4 tsp	onion powder	1 mL
1/4 tsp	garlic powder	1 mL
1/4 tsp	cornstarch	1 mL

1. In work bowl fitted with metal blade, process brown sugar, chili powder, paprika, garlic salt, sea salt, peppercorns, mustard seeds, granulated sugar, ginger, cloves, turmeric, onion powder, garlic powder and cornstarch until finely ground, about 3 minutes.

USES

Chicken: Rub about half of the mixture on a 2- to 3-lb (1 to 1.5 kg) whole chicken. Let stand at room temperature for 20 minutes. Bake in a preheated 350°F (180°C) oven or barbecue chicken until an instant-read thermometer inserted in the thigh reaches 180°F (82°C), about 15 minutes per pound (33 minutes per kilogram).

Ribs: I like to parboil my pork ribs first in a boiling pot of water for 5 minutes. Then place the ribs in a single layer on a baking sheet and cover with an even coating of the Hot and Spicy BBQ Rub, about 1/4 cup (50 mL) per full rack. Cover and let stand in the refrigerator for 45 minutes. Bake ribs in a preheated 300°F (150°C) oven until fork tender, 75 to 90 minutes.

Drunken Fresh Herb Marinade

I call this drunken because it has tequila in the marinade. See below right for the many uses for this flavorful marinade.

Tip

Make sure to use only the leaves of the tarragon and not the stems, which can taste bitter and woody.

Variation

Use orange or lemon juice in place of the lime.

3	cloves garlic	3
¼ cup	sprigs fresh tarragon (see Tip, left)	50 mL
1	serrano chile pepper	1
¼ cup	freshly squeezed lime juice	50 mL
3 tbsp	tequila	45 mL
1 tsp	salt	5 mL
¼ cup	olive oil	50 mL

1. In work bowl fitted with metal blade, process garlic, tarragon and chile until smooth. With the motor running, add lime juice, tequila and salt through the feed tube. Process for 1 minute. With the motor running, slowly drizzle oil through the feed tube until completely incorporated. Transfer to a bowl.

USES

Chicken Breasts: Marinate 4 chicken breasts in the mixture in the refrigerator for at least 45 minutes. Grill on a barbecue preheated to medium or bake in preheated 400°F (200°C) oven until chicken is no longer pink inside, 20 to 25 minutes.

Scallops: Marinate 1 lb (500 g) fresh sea scallops in the mixture for at least 10 minutes or up to 30 minutes. Grill on a barbecue preheated to medium until light brown, 3 to 5 minutes per side.

Vegetables

Pumpkin Purée 86

Grilled Portobello Mushrooms
    with Balsamic Vinegar 87

Portobello Mushroom Lasagna 88

Potato Cheese Soufflé 90

Potatoes au Gratin 92

Tomato Basil Tart. 93

Vegetable Almond Medley. 94

Eggplant Parmesan 96

Roasted Vegetables 97

Pecan Yams. 98

Pumpkin Purée

*I recall as a child asking
my grandmother if she
used real pumpkins in
her pie. She looked at
me like I was crazy.
"Why, when you can
just buy the can? It's so
easy," she would say.
I don't think she had a
food processor to make
the job easy!*

Tips
Make sure you purchase
a sugar or pie pumpkin
and not a jack-o'-lantern,
which has been bred
with thick walls to carve
and does not have much
flavor. You can ask your
produce manager to
order you one or shop at
a farmer's market. You'll
be delighted at the small
amount of seeds in the
sugar pumpkin.

Place the plastic bags
of frozen pulp in the
refrigerator a day prior
to use to thaw and
they'll be ready when
you need them.

- *Preheat oven to 375°F (190°C)*
- *Large rimmed baking sheet*

6 lb	sugar or pie pumpkin (see Tips, left)	3 kg
1/4 cup	unsalted butter, softened	50 mL
1/2 tsp	salt	2 mL

1. Cut pumpkin in half and remove stem. Scoop out seeds and membranes. Discard. Butter inside of pumpkin. Sprinkle with salt. Place skin side up on baking sheet. Bake in preheated oven until fork tender, 1 1/2 to 2 hours.

2. Let pumpkin cool for at least 30 minutes. Scoop out soft flesh and place in work bowl fitted with metal blade. Process until smooth, about 2 minutes. You may have to do this in batches because some pumpkins produce more pulp. Let cool completely. Divide mixture into 2-cup (500 mL) amounts, place in plastic bags and freeze for up to 9 months (see Tips, left).

Grilled Portobello Mushrooms with Balsamic Vinegar

These mushrooms are great as a side dish or placed between hamburger buns for a vegetarian main dish.

Tip

Purchase your mushrooms the day you are going to use them.

Variation

You can sprinkle 8 oz (250 g) freshly grated Parmesan cheese over the mushrooms about 5 minutes before they are done.

- *Preheat oven to 350°F (180°C)*
- *8-cup (2 L) baking dish*

10	portobello mushrooms, quartered (about 1½ lbs/750 g) (see Tip, left)	10
¼ cup	packed fresh basil leaves (see Tip, page 20)	50 mL
2 tbsp	balsamic vinegar	25 mL
2 tsp	salt	10 mL
¼ cup	olive oil	50 mL

1. In work bowl fitted with slicing blade, slice mushrooms. Transfer to baking dish and arrange in layers.

2. In same work bowl fitted with metal blade, add basil leaves, vinegar and salt. Process until fairly smooth, about 30 seconds. With the motor running, slowly drizzle oil through the feed tube until completely incorporated. Pour over mushrooms. Bake in preheated oven until soft to the touch, 15 to 20 minutes.

Portobello Mushroom Lasagna

You will be rewarded for the cost and time required to make this recipe when you receive all the accolades from your guests. It is a version I enjoyed at my millennium dinner celebration with friends.

Tips

Cover and reheat any leftovers in preheated 350°F (180°C) oven until hot throughout, 20 to 25 minutes.

Ask your produce manager how fresh the mushrooms are. Purchase them the day you will use them.

Use a deep baking pan or roasting pan to ensure the assembled lasagna does not fill the pan more than two-thirds full because the noodles will expand while baking.

- *Preheat oven to 425°F (220°C)*
- *13-by 9-inch (3 L) metal baking pan, at least 2 1/2 inches (6 cm) deep, buttered*

4 oz	Parmesan cheese, cut into chunks	125 g
12 oz	provolone cheese, cut into chunks	375 g
1/2	onion, cut in half	1/2
1 tbsp	olive oil	15 mL
1 1/4 lbs	portobello mushrooms, stems removed	625 g
1 tbsp	freshly squeezed lemon juice	15 mL
1 1/2 tbsp	unsalted butter	22 mL
1 1/2 tbsp	all-purpose flour	22 mL
4 cups	whipping (35%) cream, at room temperature	1 L
1	package (10 oz/300 g) oven-ready lasagna noodles, divided	1
1	package (10 oz/300 g) frozen spinach, thawed and drained, divided	1
8 oz	ricotta cheese	250 g

1. In work bowl fitted with metal blade, with the motor running, add Parmesan cheese through the feed tube and process until finely grated. Transfer to a bowl. Set aside.

2. In work bowl fitted with shredding blade, shred provolone cheese. Transfer to another bowl. Set aside.

3. In work bowl fitted with slicing blade, slice onion. Heat oil in a large pot over medium heat. Add onion and sauté until opaque, about 5 minutes.

4. Meanwhile, in work bowl fitted with slicing blade, slice mushrooms. Add to pot with onions and steam, covered, until tender, for 5 minutes. Transfer mixture to a bowl. Set aside.

5. In same pot over medium heat, cook lemon juice and butter until butter is fully melted, about 1 minute. Whisk in flour and cook, stirring, until light brown and thick, about 2 minutes. Gradually whisk in cream and cook, whisking constantly, until mixture starts to thicken, about 5 minutes. Set aside.

6. Placed one-third of the noodles in a single layer in prepared baking dish, trimming to fit as necessary. Spread half of the spinach evenly over noodles. Then spread half of the mushroom mixture, one-third of the Parmesan cheese, one-third of the provolone cheese and one-third of the cream mixture. Add half of remaining noodles in a layer. Spread with remaining spinach, then mushroom mixture, half of the remaining Parmesan, half of the remaining provolone and half of the remaining cream mixture. Place remaining noodles on top and press down with your hand to even it all out. Add remaining Parmesan, provolone and cream mixture. Dollop ricotta by spoonfuls on top so you have 10 dollops in 5 rows by 2 rows.

7. Bake in preheated oven, covered, for 45 minutes or until noodles are tender. Uncover and bake 10 minutes more until hot and bubbling and top is browned. Let lasagna stand for 15 minutes. Serve hot.

Potato Cheese Soufflé

Vegetable soufflés are simple to master. If the soufflé falls before you can serve it, call it a baked vegetable dish instead!

Tips

You can use ½ cup (125 mL) prepared instant potatoes in a pinch. Prepare according to package directions.

If your food processor has a whip attachment, you can use it to whip the egg whites. Make sure the work bowl is clean, free of any grease and dry for the best volume.

Variation

Try a blue cheese in place of the Romano to add some bite to your soufflé.

- *Preheat oven to 375°F (190°C)*
- *6-cup (1.5 L) soufflé dish, sprayed with nonstick spray*

1	small russet potato, peeled and cut into quarters	1
4 oz	Romano cheese, cut into chunks	125 g
2	cloves garlic	2
2½ tbsp	unsalted butter	32 mL
¼ cup	all-purpose flour	50 mL
1 cup	milk	250 mL
Pinch	salt	Pinch
Pinch	ground white pepper	Pinch
4	egg yolks	4
5	egg whites	5

1. In a saucepan, cover potato with cold water. Bring to a boil over high heat. Reduce heat and boil gently until tender, about 15 minutes. Drain and set aside to cool.

2. In work bowl fitted with metal blade, with the motor running, add Romano cheese through the feed tube and process until grated. Transfer to a bowl.

3. In same work bowl fitted with metal blade, add potato and garlic. Process until smooth, about 45 seconds. Set aside.

4. In a clean saucepan over low heat, melt butter. Add flour and cook, stirring, for 1 minute to make a roux. In a steady stream, whisk in milk. Mix in reserved cheese, potato mixture, salt and white pepper. Add egg yolks, one at a time, whisking well between each addition. Transfer to a large bowl.

5. In a large bowl, using an electric mixer, whip egg whites until soft but firm peaks form. Carefully fold egg whites into cheese mixture, trying not to deflate mixture, just until no whites are visible. Do not overmix. Transfer mixture to prepared soufflé dish, smoothing top. Bake in preheated oven until soufflé has risen and browned slightly on top, about 30 minutes. Do not be tempted to open the oven while soufflé is baking or it will fall.

Potatoes au Gratin

I love these potatoes when their flavors are allowed to develop. Don't hesitate to serve them a few days after making them.

Tip

If the milk is cold it will take a lot longer to cook and thicken the mixture. Measure the amount needed and leave on the counter for at least an hour prior to making.

Variation

Try different cheeses, such as Gouda or Edam, in place of the Cheddar.

● *Preheat oven to 400°F (200°C)*
● *13-by 9-inch (3 L) baking dish, buttered*

10 oz	Cheddar cheese, cut into chunks	300 g
6	russet potatoes, peeled and cut in half (about 1 ½ lbs/750 g)	6
1 ½	sweet onions, quartered	1 ½
Pinch	salt	Pinch
Pinch	freshly ground black pepper	Pinch
Pinch	freshly ground nutmeg	Pinch
⅓ cup	unsalted butter	75 mL
¼ cup	all-purpose flour	50 mL
3 cups	milk, at room temperature (see Tip, left)	750 mL

1. In work bowl fitted with shredding blade, shred cheese. Transfer to a bowl.

2. In same work bowl fitted with slicing blade, slice potatoes. Transfer to a small bowl. In same work bowl, slice onions.

3. In prepared baking dish, layer half of the potatoes and then onion slices. Top with remaining potatoes. Season with salt, black pepper and nutmeg. Set aside.

4. In a saucepan over medium heat, melt butter. Whisk in flour, stirring constantly, for 1 minute. Gradually whisk in milk. Cook, stirring constantly, until mixture is thickened, about 5 minutes. Remove from heat. Stir in cheese all at once and continue stirring until cheese is slightly melted, 30 to 60 seconds. Pour cheese mixture over potatoes. Cover baking dish with foil.

5. Bake in preheated oven until bubbling and a fork inserted into center is soft, 75 to 90 minutes. If you would like the top to have a nice brown look, remove the foil for the last 5 minutes of baking.

Tomato Basil Tart

This is a great savory tart to have in your freezer for a fast appetizer or main dish.

Tip

If you don't let tomatoes drain on paper towels the tart will be very watery.

Variation

You can try some of the colorful heirloom varieties of tomatoes in place of the Roma varieties.

● *Preheat oven to 375°F (190°C)*

½	recipe Savory Buttery Tart Pastry (see recipe variation, page 139)	½
6 oz	mozzarella cheese, cut into chunks	175 g
3 oz	Romano cheese, cut into chunks	90 g
4	cloves garlic	4
½ cup	Traditional Mayonnaise (see recipe, page 36) or store-bought	125 mL
⅛ tsp	ground white pepper	0.5 mL
⅛ tsp	salt	0.5 mL
1 cup	loosely packed fresh basil leaves	250 mL
5	Roma tomatoes, cored	5

1. In work bowl fitted with shredding blade, shred mozzarella. Sprinkle ½ cup (125 mL) cheese over tart shell. Set aside. Transfer remaining cheese to a bowl.

2. In same work bowl fitted with metal blade, with the motor running, add Romano cheese and garlic through the feed tube and process until finely chopped. Transfer to bowl with mozzarella. Add mayonnaise, white pepper and salt. Set aside.

3. In same work bowl fitted with metal blade, add basil and process until coarsely chopped, about 10 seconds. Transfer to another bowl. Set aside.

4. In same work bowl fitted with slicing blade, slice tomatoes. Place in a single layer on paper towels and drain for 10 minutes.

5. Arrange tomato slices over cheese in tart shell. Sprinkle basil over tomatoes. Spread cheese mixture evenly over basil to cover. Bake in preheated oven until top is golden and bubbling, 35 to 40 minutes. Serve warm.

Vegetable Almond Medley

I created this recipe with all the leftover vegetables I had after the holidays.

Tip

I like to use low-sodium soy sauce because the regular kind is too salty.

Variation

Add ½ cup (125 mL) grated Romano cheese to the topping.

- *Preheat oven to 400°F (200°C)*
- *8-cup (2 L) baking dish, buttered*

3 lbs	mixed vegetables, such as carrots, radishes, turnips and broccoli	1.5 kg
1	onion, quartered	1
2	cloves garlic	2
5 tbsp	unsalted butter, divided	75 mL
1½ cups	toasted almonds, divided	375 mL
2 cups	vegetable stock, divided	500 mL
3 tbsp	all-purpose flour	45 mL
1 tbsp	low-sodium soy sauce (see Tip, left)	15 mL
½ tsp	dry mustard powder	2 mL
½ cup	Fresh Bread Crumbs (see recipe, page 26)	125 mL

1. In work bowl fitted with slicing blade slice mixed vegetables in batches. Transfer to a bowl. Set aside.

2. In same work bowl fitted with slicing blade, slice onion. Transfer to another bowl. Set aside.

3. Replace slicing blade with metal blade and pulse garlic until chopped, about 5 times. Transfer to bowl with onion.

4. In a large saucepan over medium heat, melt 2 tbsp (25 mL) butter. Add onion and garlic and sauté until onion is opaque, 7 to 12 minutes. Add mixed vegetables and sauté until soft, 8 to 12 minutes. Place in prepared baking dish.

5. In same work bowl fitted with metal blade, add 1 cup (250 mL) almonds and $\frac{1}{2}$ cup (125 mL) vegetable stock. Process until smooth. Set aside.

6. In same saucepan over medium heat, melt remaining butter. Add flour and cook, whisking until thick, about 1 minute. Gradually whisk in remaining vegetable stock and almond mixture. Add soy sauce and dry mustard and cook, stirring, until thickened, about 10 minutes. Pour over vegetables in baking dish. Sprinkle remaining $\frac{1}{2}$ cup (125 mL) almonds and bread crumbs over top. Bake in preheated oven until heated through and top is light brown, 15 to 20 minutes.

Eggplant Parmesan

Eggplant technically is a fruit like a tomato, but most of us think of it as a vegetable. This dish will be the vegetarian's favorite at a potluck.

Variation

You can also add a layer of 3 sliced Roma tomatoes on top of the eggplant.

● *Preheat oven to 400°F (200°C)*
● *13-by 9-inch (3 L) baking dish, sprayed with nonstick spray*

2 oz	Parmesan cheese, cut into chunks	60 g
8 oz	mozzarella cheese, cut into chunks	250 g
1	large eggplant, peeled and cut into quarters (about 2 lbs/1 kg)	1
¾ cup	vegetable oil	175 mL
2 cups	Tomato Sauce (see recipe, page 179) or store-bought	500 mL
½ tsp	dried basil leaves	2 mL
½ tsp	garlic powder	2 mL

1. In work bowl fitted with metal blade, with the motor running, add Parmesan cheese through the feed tube and process until finely grated. Transfer to a bowl. Set aside.

2. In same work bowl fitted with shredding blade, shred mozzarella cheese. Transfer to another bowl. Set aside.

3. In same work bowl fitted with slicing blade, slice eggplant.

4. Heat oil in a skillet over medium heat. Add eggplant, in batches as necessary, and sauté until lightly cooked on both sides, 3 to 4 minutes. Place in a single layer on paper towels and drain.

5. Place one-third of the eggplant in a layer over bottom of prepared baking pan. Spread with one-third each of the tomato sauce, basil, garlic powder, Parmesan cheese and mozzarella. Repeat layering two more times with remaining ingredients, finishing with cheeses on top. Bake in preheated oven, uncovered, until heated through and cheese is melted, 15 to 20 minutes. Serve hot.

Fast and Easy Meat Loaf (page 77)

Overleaf: Honey Whole Wheat Sunflower Bread (page 102), Sun-Dried Tomato Pesto Bread (page 106) and Cheddar Cheese Rolls (page 110)

Roasted Vegetables

This is one of the most flavorful dishes you'll ever serve, and it takes no time to make.

Tip

If any of the vegetables are out of season substitute whatever is in season such as zucchini, yellowneck squash or turnip. Use this recipe as guide.

Variation

You can make vegetable soup with these roasted vegetables. Place vegetables and 3 cups (750 mL) water in a saucepan. Bring to a simmer over high heat and simmer for 20 minutes. Strain, discarding vegetables.

- *Preheat oven to 400°F (200°C)*
- *Roasting pan, lined with parchment paper*

1	onion, quartered	1
8 oz	new potatoes, quartered, if large (about 3)	250 g
8 oz	yams, peeled and quartered, if large (about 2) (see Tip, page 98)	250 g
2	large carrots, cut into 3-inch (7.5 cm) lengths	2
1 cup	radishes, stems removed (about 8 oz/250 g)	250 mL
1	red bell pepper, sliced in half and seeded	1
2 tbsp	olive oil	25 mL
1 tsp	fresh thyme leaves	5 mL
1 tsp	fresh oregano leaves	5 mL
1/2 tsp	salt	2 mL
1/2 tsp	ground white pepper	2 mL

1. In work bowl fitted with slicing blade, one vegetable at a time, slice onion, potatoes, yams, carrots, radishes and bell pepper. Transfer to a large bowl and toss with olive oil, thyme, oregano, salt and white pepper.

2. Transfer to prepared roasting pan in a single layer. Roast in preheated oven, stirring every 10 to 15 minutes, until light brown and tender, 45 to 60 minutes. Serve hot.

Potatoes au Gratin (page 92)

Pecan Yams

Serves 8

These yams are a staple on my holiday table. I hope they'll be on yours, too.

Tip

Although technically not the same thing, yams and sweet potatoes are interchangeable in this recipe.

Variation

Add ½ cup (125 mL) drained crushed pineapple when you add the yams for an island flavor.

● *Preheat oven to 350°F (180°C)*
● *13-by 9-inch (3 L) baking dish, buttered*

2 lbs	yams, peeled and cut to fit in feed tube	1 kg
½ cup	unsalted butter	125 mL
1 cup	lightly packed brown sugar	250 mL
1 tsp	ground cinnamon	5 mL
¼ tsp	freshly ground nutmeg	1 mL
1 cup	pecan halves	250 mL

1. In work bowl fitted with slicing blade, slice yams. Transfer to a saucepan over medium heat and fill with cold water to cover. Bring to a boil. Reduce heat and simmer until fork tender, 20 to 25 minutes. Do not let the water boil. Drain well and transfer to prepared baking dish.

2. In same saucepan over medium heat, melt butter. Add brown sugar, cinnamon and nutmeg and heat until melted. Set aside.

3. Replace slicing blade with metal blade and pulse pecans until coarsely chopped. Add to sugar mixture and combine. Pour over yams and bake in preheated oven until bubbling, 20 to 25 minutes. Serve hot.

Yeast Breads and Rolls

California Wine and Cheese Bread 100

Honey Whole Wheat Sunflower Bread 102

Fresh Tarragon Dill Bread. 104

Sun-Dried Tomato Pesto Bread. 106

Potato Rolls 108

Cheddar Cheese Rolls 110

Whole Wheat Rolls 112

Crusty French Rolls. 114

Fast and Easy Pizza Dough. 116

California Wine and Cheese Bread

Makes 1 loaf

The white wine gives this bread a light flavor and great texture.

Tips
Make sure you have plenty of flour on hand. Never try to make a recipe with the exact amount of flour called for in the recipe because most likely you'll end up needing more. If you are making bread in New Orleans, for instance, where the humidity is high, you'll need additional flour to "soak up" the extra moisture, whereas in Phoenix or Edmonton you may need less. This is why the flours are always a variable or an approximation.

Check your food processor instruction manual to see if this amount of flour is suitable for use with the dough blade. It may work better with the regular metal blade.

- *Instant-read thermometer*
- *Baking sheet, lined with parchment paper*

¼ cup	dry white wine	50 mL
¼ cup	water	50 mL
2 tbsp	unsalted butter	25 mL
4 oz	Monterey Jack cheese, cut into chunks	125 g
2½ cups	bread flour, divided (approx.)	625 mL
1¾ tsp	granulated sugar	9 mL
½ tsp	salt	2 mL
1	package (¼ oz/8 g) quick-rising (instant) dry yeast	1
1	egg	1

1. In a small saucepan over medium heat, bring wine, water and butter to a simmer until an instant-read thermometer registers approximately 120° to 130°F (50° to 55°C), about 3 minutes. Do not let boil.

2. Meanwhile, in work bowl fitted with shredding blade, shred cheese. Transfer to a bowl.

3. Replace shredding blade with metal blade or metal dough blade (see Tips, left). Add 2 cups (500 mL) of the flour, sugar, salt and yeast and process until well combined, about 15 seconds. With the motor running, slowly pour hot wine mixture through the feed tube into work bowl. Add egg and cheese and process until blended, about 20 seconds. With the motor continuing to run, spoon additional flour through the feed tube into mixture, about ¼ cup (50 mL) at a time, until dough pulls away from sides and begins to gather and a soft, not sticky, dough forms, about 90 seconds.

Variation

You can replace the wine with white grape juice or milk.

4. Remove dough from work bowl and place on a floured surface. Knead until dough is smooth and elastic, 3 to 5 minutes. Shape into a ball. Transfer to a large oiled bowl and turn to coat all over. Cover loosely with plastic wrap. Let dough rise in a warm, draft-free place until double in volume, about 45 to 90 minutes, depending on the humidity and heat factors.

5. Preheat the oven to 375°F (190°C). Punch down dough and form into a round loaf. Place on prepared baking sheet. Cover with a towel and let rest in a warm, draft-free place until it rises slightly, 20 to 30 minutes. Bake in preheated oven until light brown, 30 to 40 minutes. Let cool on wire rack.

Honey Whole Wheat Sunflower Bread

Makes 2 loaves

This is my favorite bread. The honey makes the texture so soft and smooth.

Tip

Sometimes the honey sinks to the bottom of the milk mixture. Make sure you use a heatproof spatula to remove it all from the pan.

Variation

Add ¼ tsp (1 mL) ground cardamom to the flour mixture.

- *Instant-read thermometer*
- *Baking sheet, lined with parchment paper*

1½ cups	milk	375 mL
1½ tbsp	unsalted butter	22 mL
2 tbsp	liquid honey	25 mL
2 cups	all-purpose flour, divided (approx.)	500 mL
2 cups	whole wheat flour	500 mL
1	package (¼ oz/8 g) quick-rising (instant) dry yeast	1
1 tsp	salt	5 mL
½ cup	roasted unsalted sunflower seeds	125 mL

1. In a small saucepan over medium heat, bring milk, butter and honey to a simmer until an instant-read thermometer registers approximately 120° to 130°F (50° to 55°C), about 3 minutes. Do not let boil.

2. Meanwhile, in work bowl fitted with metal dough blade, process 1½ cups (375 mL) of the all-purpose flour, the whole wheat flour, yeast and salt until well combined, about 15 seconds. With the motor running, slowly pour hot milk mixture through the feed tube into work bowl. With the motor continuing to run, spoon additional all-purpose flour through the feed tube, about ¼ cup (50 mL) at a time, until dough pulls away from sides and begins to gather and a soft, not sticky, dough forms, about 90 seconds. Add sunflower seeds and pulse 5 times.

3. Remove from work bowl and place on a floured surface. Knead until dough is smooth and elastic, 3 to 5 minutes. Shape into a ball. Transfer to a large oiled bowl and turn to coat all over. Cover loosely with plastic wrap. Let dough rise in a warm, draft-free place until double in volume, about 45 to 90 minutes, depending on the humidity and heat factors.

4. Preheat the oven to 350°F (180°C). Punch down dough and form into two round loaves. Place on prepared baking sheet, at least 2 inches (5 cm) apart. Cover with a towel and let rest in a warm, draft-free place until they rise slightly, 20 to 30 minutes. Bake in preheated oven until light brown, 30 to 40 minutes. Let cool on wire rack.

Fresh Tarragon Dill Bread

Makes 2 loaves

The taste of fresh herbs in this bread reminds me of the gardens of the south of France.

Tip

The bread will have a green tinge to it because of the herbs. Do not use dry herbs because they will look like specks of black in the dough.

Variation

Try using rosemary or thyme in place of the dill and tarragon.

- *Instant-read thermometer*
- *Baking sheet, lined with parchment paper*

1¾ cups	milk	425 mL
2 tbsp	unsalted butter	25 mL
½ cup	loosely packed fresh parsley, stems removed	125 mL
2	cloves garlic	2
2 tsp	fresh dill	10 mL
2 tsp	fresh tarragon leaves	10 mL
4½ cups	all-purpose flour (approx.)	1.125 L
2 tbsp	granulated sugar	25 mL
2	packages (each ¼ oz/8 g) quick-rising (instant) dry yeast	2
2½ tsp	salt	12 mL

1. In a saucepan over medium heat, bring milk and butter to a simmer until an instant-read thermometer registers approximately 120° to 130°F (50° to 55°C), about 3 minutes. Do not let boil.

2. Meanwhile, in work bowl fitted with metal blade, pulse parsley, garlic, dill and tarragon until finely chopped, about 20 times. Transfer to a small bowl.

3. In same work bowl fitted with metal dough blade, process 3 cups (750 mL) of the flour, sugar, yeast and salt for 15 seconds. With the motor running, slowly pour hot milk mixture through the feed tube into work bowl. Then add herb mixture, pulsing 10 times. With the motor continuing to run, add additional flour through the feed tube, ¼ cup (50 mL) at a time, until dough pulls away from sides and begins to gather and a soft, not sticky, dough forms, about 90 seconds.

4. Remove dough from work bowl and place on a floured surface. Knead until dough is smooth and elastic, 3 to 5 minutes. Shape into a ball. Transfer to a large oiled bowl and turn to coat all over. Cover loosely with plastic wrap. Let dough rise in a warm, draft-free place until double in volume, about 45 to 90 minutes, depending on the humidity and heat factors.

5. Preheat the oven to 350°F (180°C). Punch down dough and form into two round loaves. Place on prepared baking sheet, at least 2 inches (5 cm) apart. Cover with a towel and let rest in a warm, draft-free place until they rise slightly, 20 to 30 minutes. Bake in preheated oven until light brown, 30 to 40 minutes. Let cool on wire rack.

Sun-Dried Tomato Pesto Bread

Makes 2 loaves

This is a great bread to have with a big helping of pasta!

Tip

If you can only find sun-dried tomatoes that are not packed in oil, make sure you soften them by placing them in a dish of hot water and soak until softened, about 30 minutes. Drain and pat dry before using.

Variation

If fresh basil is unavailable or too expensive, use Italian parsley instead.

- *Instant-read thermometer*
- *Baking sheet, lined with parchment paper*

⅓ cup	oil-packed sun-dried tomatoes, drained (see Tip, left)	75 mL
⅓ cup	packed fresh basil leaves	75 mL
¾ cup	milk	175 mL
2 tbsp	unsalted butter	25 mL
3 cups	bread flour (approx.)	750 mL
I	package (¼ oz/8 g) quick-rising (instant) dry yeast	I
I tsp	granulated sugar	5 mL
½ tsp	salt	2 mL
I	egg	I

1. In work bowl fitted with metal blade, process sun-dried tomatoes and basil until smooth, about 2 minutes. Transfer to a bowl.

2. In a small saucepan over medium heat, bring milk and butter to a simmer until an instant-read thermometer registers approximately 120° to 130°F (50° to 55°C), about 3 minutes. Do not let boil.

3. Meanwhile, in clean work bowl fitted with metal dough blade, add 2 cups (500 mL) of the flour, yeast, sugar and salt and process until well combined, about 15 seconds. With the motor running, slowly pour hot milk mixture through the feed tube into the work bowl. Add egg and process until incorporated, about 20 seconds. With the motor continuing to run, add sun-dried tomato mixture until incorporated. With the motor running, spoon additional flour through the feed tube, ¼ cup (50 mL) at a time, until dough pulls away from sides and begins to gather and a soft, not sticky, dough forms, about 90 seconds.

4. Remove dough from work bowl and place on a floured surface. Knead until dough is smooth and elastic, 3 to 5 minutes. Shape into a ball. Transfer to a large oiled bowl and turn to coat all over. Cover loosely with plastic wrap. Let dough rise in a warm, draft-free place until double in volume, about 45 to 90 minutes, depending on humidity and heat factors.

5. Preheat the oven to 350°F (180°C). Punch down dough and form into two round loaves. Place on prepared baking sheet, at least 2 inches (5 cm) apart. Cover with a towel and let rest in a warm, draft-free place until they rise slightly, 20 to 30 minutes. Bake in preheated oven until light brown, 30 to 40 minutes. Let cool on wire rack.

Potato Rolls

Makes 12

These rolls add great flavor to any meal. They're perfect for a holiday table.

Tip

If you do not have a potato handy you can use instant potatoes. Prepare according to package directions to make ⅓ cup (75 mL).

Variation

Roll dough into 36 rolls and place 3 rounds in each cup of a greased 12-cup muffin tin. You now have cloverleaf rolls. Bake in preheated 350°F (180°C) oven until light brown on top, 16 to 20 minutes.

- *Instant-read thermometer*
- *Baking sheet, lined with parchment paper*

½	russet potato, baked and peeled	½
¾ cup	milk	175 mL
2 tbsp	unsalted butter, softened	25 mL
1½ tbsp	liquid honey	22 mL
3 cups	bread flour, divided (approx.)	750 mL
1	package (¼ oz/8 g) quick-rising (instant) dry yeast	1
1 tsp	salt	5 mL

1. In the work bowl fitted with metal blade, process potato until soft and smooth. Measure out ⅓ cup (75 mL). Transfer to a small bowl. (Use any remaining potato for another use.)

2. In a saucepan over medium heat, bring milk, butter and honey to a simmer until an instant-read thermometer registers approximately 120° to 130°F (50° to 55°C), about 3 minutes. Do not let boil.

3. Meanwhile, in work bowl fitted with metal dough blade, process 2 cups (500 mL) of the flour, yeast and salt until well combined, about 15 seconds. With the motor running, slowly add hot milk mixture through the feed tube. With the motor continuing to run, add potato, one-third at a time, then spoon additional flour through the feed tube, ¼ cup (50 mL) at a time, until dough starts to pull away from sides and begins to gather and a soft, not sticky, dough forms.

4. Remove dough from work bowl and place on a floured surface. Knead until dough is smooth and elastic, 3 to 5 minutes. Shape into a ball. Transfer to a large oiled bowl and turn to coat all over. Cover loosely with plastic wrap. Let dough rise in a warm, draft-free place until double in volume, about 45 to 90 minutes, depending on humidity and heat factors.

5. Preheat oven to 350°F (180°C). Punch down dough and form into 12 round rolls. Transfer to prepared baking sheet touching side by side so they join together when rising. With tips of a pair of kitchen shears, cut a shallow slit in the top of each roll. Dust with additional flour. Cover with a towel and let rest in a warm, draft-free place until they rise slightly, 15 to 20 minutes. Bake in preheated oven until light brown on top, 16 to 20 minutes. Let cool on wire rack. Pull apart to serve.

Cheddar Cheese Rolls

Serve these rich rolls with a hearty chowder. It's a great combo during the winter.

Tip

Sugar adds color to the final baked rolls and salt balances the flavor. Do not omit.

Variation

Try Swiss or Monterey Jack cheese in place of the cheddar cheese.

- *Instant-read thermometer*
- *Baking sheet, lined with parchment paper*

6 oz	Cheddar cheese, cut into chunks	175 g
¾ cup	water	175 mL
1½ tsp	unsalted butter, softened	7 mL
3½ cups	bread flour, divided (approx.)	875 mL
1 tbsp	granulated sugar (see Tip, left)	15 mL
1	package (¼ oz/8 g) quick-rising (instant) dry yeast	1
1 tsp	salt	5 mL
1	egg	1

1. In work bowl fitted with shredding blade, shred cheese. Transfer to a small bowl. Transfer 2 tbsp (25 mL) to a separate bowl, cover and refrigerate. Set remaining cheese aside.

2. In a small saucepan, bring water and butter to a simmer until an instant-read thermometer registers approximately 120° to 130°F (50° to 55°C), about 3 minutes. Do not let boil.

3. Meanwhile, in same work bowl fitted with metal dough blade, process 2 cups (500 mL) of the flour, sugar, yeast and salt until well combined, about 15 seconds. With the motor running, slowly add hot water mixture through the feed tube into work bowl. Add egg and all but 2 tbsp (25 mL) cheese and process until incorporated, about 5 seconds. With the motor continuing to run, spoon additional flour through the feed tube, ¼ cup (50 mL) at time, until dough starts to pull away from sides and begins to gather and a soft, not sticky, dough forms.

4. Remove from work bowl and place on a floured surface. Knead until dough is smooth and elastic, 3 to 5 minutes. Shape into a ball. Transfer to a large oiled bowl and turn to coat all over. Cover loosely with plastic wrap. Let dough rise in a warm, draft-free place until double in volume, about 45 to 90 minutes, depending on humidity and heat factors.

5. Preheat oven to 375°F (190°C). Punch down dough, form into 12 round rolls and place on prepared baking sheet, about 2 inches (5 cm) apart. Top with grated cheese. Cover with a towel and let rest in a warm, draft-free place until they rise slightly, 15 to 20 minutes. Top with reserved refrigerated grated cheese. Bake in preheated oven until light brown and cheese is bubbling, 12 to 18 minutes. Let cool on wire rack.

Whole Wheat Rolls

I like to pair these rolls with a hearty beef stew or chili.

Tip

To create even size rolls, I suggest cutting the dough in quarters, and then cutting those into thirds resulting in 12 rolls.

Variation

Brush tops with water or butter and sprinkle rolls with ½ cup (125 mL) chopped walnuts after shaping.

● *Instant-read thermometer*
● *Baking sheet, lined with parchment paper*

1 cup	milk	250 mL
1 tbsp	unsalted butter	15 mL
1½ tbsp	pure maple syrup	22 mL
1¾ cups	all-purpose flour, divided (approx.)	425 mL
1¾ cups	whole wheat flour, divided (approx.)	425 mL
1	package (¼ oz/8 g) quick-rising (instant) dry yeast	1
1 tsp	salt	5 mL

1. In a saucepan over medium heat, bring milk, butter and maple syrup to a simmer until an instant-read thermometer registers approximately 120° to 130°F (50° to 55°C), about 3 minutes. Do not let boil.

2. Meanwhile, in work bowl fitted with metal dough blade, process 1 cup (250 mL) each of the all-purpose flour and whole wheat flours, yeast and salt until well combined, about 15 seconds. With the motor running, slowly add hot milk mixture through the feed tube into work bowl. With the motor continuing to run, alternately spoon additional all-purpose and whole wheat flours through the feed tube, ¼ cup (50 mL) at a time, until dough starts to pull away from sides and begins to gather and a soft, not sticky, dough forms.

3. Remove from work bowl and place on a floured surface. Knead until dough is smooth and elastic, 3 to 5 minutes. Shape into a ball. Transfer to a large oiled bowl and turn to coat all over. Cover loosely with plastic wrap. Let dough rise in a warm, draft-free place until double in volume, about 45 to 90 minutes, depending on humidity and heat factors.

4. Preheat oven to 350°F (180°C). Punch down dough and form into 12 rolls. Transfer to prepared baking sheet, about 2 inches (5 cm) apart. Cover with a towel and let rest in a warm, draft-free place until they rise slightly, 20 to 30 minutes. Bake in preheated oven until light brown, 18 to 22 minutes. Let cool on wire rack.

Crusty French Rolls

When I worked for Marriott Hotels we would make thousands and thousands of French rolls for banquets — all hand-rolled. Here's a recipe that only requires you to make a dozen.

Tip

Use a misting bottle instead of a pastry brush to avoid flattening the dough.

Variation

You can form the dough into 4 rounds and use them as soup bowls. Increase baking time to 24 to 30 minutes. Hollow out after they have been baked and cooled.

- *Instant-read thermometer*
- *Baking sheet, lined with parchment paper*

1 1/4 cups	water, divided	300 mL
3 1/2 cups	all-purpose flour, divided (approx.)	875 mL
1	package (1/4 oz/8 g) quick-rising (instant) dry yeast	1
1 tbsp	granulated sugar	15 mL
1 tsp	salt	5 mL

1. In a saucepan over medium heat, bring 1 cup (250 mL) of the water to a simmer until an instant-read thermometer registers approximately 120° to 130°F (50° to 55°C). Do not let boil.

2. Meanwhile, in work bowl fitted with metal dough blade, process 2 cups (500 mL) of the flour, yeast, sugar and salt until well combined, for 10 seconds. With the motor running, slowly add 1 cup (250 mL) warm water through the feed tube into work bowl. With the motor continuing to run, spoon additional flour through the feed tube, 1/4 cup (50 mL) at a time, until dough starts to pull away from sides and begins to gather and a soft, not sticky, dough forms.

3. Remove from work bowl and place on a floured surface. Knead until dough is smooth and elastic, 3 to 5 minutes. Shape into a ball. Transfer to a large oiled bowl and turn to coat all over. Cover loosely with plastic wrap. Let dough rise in a warm, draft-free place until double in volume, about 45 to 90 minutes, depending on humidity and heat factors.

4. Preheat oven to 400°F (200°C). Punch down dough and form into 12 round rolls. Roll out each ball into logs, like miniature hot dog buns, about $3\frac{1}{2}$ inches (8.5 cm) long. Place on prepared baking sheet, 3 inches (7.5 cm) apart. With the tips of a pair of kitchen shears, cut 3 slits along the top of each roll. Cover with a towel and let rest in a warm, draft-free place until they rise slightly, 20 to 30 minutes. Transfer remaining $\frac{1}{4}$ cup (50 mL) of the water to a misting bottle and spray dough with a fine mist (see Tip, page 114). Bake in preheated oven until light brown, 18 to 22 minutes. Let cool on wire rack.

Fast and Easy Pizza Dough

Sprinkle this easy dough with your favorite toppings, such as cheeses, cooked chicken, salami and roasted vegetables, to create your very own signature pizzas.

Tip

You can make the dough to the end of Step 2 up to 3 days ahead. Refrigerate until ready to use. Let warm to room temperature before shaping in Step 3.

Variation

Replace half of the flour with whole wheat flour for a whole wheat crust. Don't replace all of the flour with whole wheat or you will have a brick.

- *Baking sheet, dusted with 2 tsp (10 mL) cornmeal*
- *Instant-read thermometer*

1 cup	milk	250 mL
1 tbsp	unsalted butter, softened	15 mL
3 cups	all-purpose flour, divided (approx.)	750 mL
1 tbsp	granulated sugar	15 mL
1 1/4 tsp	salt	6 mL
1	package (1/4 oz/8 g) quick-rising (instant) dry yeast	1

1. In a saucepan over medium heat, bring milk and butter to a simmer until an instant-read thermometer registers approximately 120° to 130°F (50° to 55°C), about 3 minutes. Do not let boil.

2. Meanwhile, in work bowl fitted with metal dough blade, process 2 cups (500 mL) of the flour, sugar, salt and yeast until well combined, about 10 seconds. With the motor running, slowly pour hot milk mixture through the feed tube into work bowl. With the motor continuing to run, spoon additional flour through the feed tube, 1/4 cup (50 mL) at a time, until dough starts to pull away from sides and begins to gather.

3. Remove from work bowl and place on a floured surface. Knead until dough is smooth and elastic, 3 to 5 minutes. Shape into a ball. Transfer to a large oiled bowl and turn to coat all over. Cover loosely with plastic wrap. Let dough rise in a warm, draft-free place until double in volume, about 45 to 90 minutes, depending on humidity and heat factors.

4. Preheat oven to 425°F (220°C). Punch down dough and cut in half. Press each out to about 1/2 inch (1 cm) thick and 10 inches (25 cm) round. Transfer to prepared baking sheet. Add your favorite toppings. For a thin crust, bake right away; for a thicker crust, let rise for 15 to 20 minutes. Bake in preheated oven until the crust is light brown on bottom, 15 to 20 minutes.

Cookies and Brownies

All-Rich Butter Cookies 118

Vanilla Sugar. 119

Lemon Citrus Cookies. 120

Orange Zest Cookies. 121

Strawberry Almond Cookies. 122

Pecan Pumpkin Harvest Cookies 123

Oatmeal Cinnamon Raisin Cookies 124

Peanut Sandwich Cookies 126

Cinnamon Apple Shortbread 128

Sugar and Spice Cookies 129

Quadruple Chocolate Chunk Cookies 130

The Perfect Fudgey Brownie 131

Chocolate Raspberry Brownies 132

All-Rich Butter Cookies

| **Makes about 36 cookies** |

Every European country feels that they have created the butter cookie. You can keep them simple or add any of the variations below for your own signature butter cookie.

Tips

Store cookies in an airtight container for up to 4 days. You can also freeze them in resealable plastic bags for up to 1 month.

Be careful not to overprocess once you have added flour to the mixture.

If you don't have vanilla sugar, mix together ¾ cup (175 mL) granulated sugar and 1 tbsp (15 mL) vanilla instead.

Variations

After you have made the dough you may stir in ½ cup (125 mL) chopped and toasted nuts, such as cashews, peanuts, walnuts or almonds, or ½ cup (125 mL) chopped milk chocolate.

● *Preheat oven to 350°F (180°C)*
● *2 baking sheets, lined with parchment paper*

1 cup	unsalted butter, softened	250 mL
¾ cup	vanilla sugar (see Tips, left, and recipe, page 119)	175 mL
3 cups	all-purpose flour	750 mL

1. In work bowl fitted with metal blade, process butter until light and creamy, about 10 seconds. Add vanilla sugar and process until incorporated, about 30 seconds. Scrape work bowl to incorporate the whole mixture. Add flour and process just until combined, about 10 seconds. If dough is very soft, transfer to a bowl and refrigerate until firm, about 20 minutes.

2. Scoop dough by heaping tablespoonfuls (15 mL) and squeeze into a ball. Place on prepared baking sheets, about 2 inches (5 cm) apart. Slightly flatten each cookie by pressing down with the palm of your hand or the bottom of a drinking glass. Bake in preheated oven until edges are firm and without color, 12 to 18 minutes. Let cool on baking sheets for 10 minutes before transferring to a wire rack to cool completely.

Vanilla Sugar

Make 2 cups (500 mL)

Put some of this sugar in your coffee and you'll feel like you're in Paris! All of the coffeehouses serve this. Also, use it in All-Rich Butter Cookies (see recipe, page 118).

Tips

Vanilla sugar keeps stored in an airtight container for up to 1 year.

This sugar is also used in many French baked goods in place of vanilla and sugar.

Variation

Add a few drops of almond extract through the feed tube while the motor is running for almond vanilla sugar.

2	whole vanilla beans	2
2 cups	granulated sugar	500 mL

1. Cut each vanilla bean in half lengthwise. Cut crosswise into slices.

2. In work bowl fitted with metal blade, process sugar and beans until very smooth, about 2 minutes.

Lemon Citrus Cookies

I like how these cookies burst with lemon. Perfect to cool you down on a warm summer day.

Tips

Store cookies in an airtight container for up to 4 days. You can also freeze them in resealable plastic bags for up to 1 month.

If you don't have lemon oil you can use $\frac{1}{2}$ tsp (2 mL) lemon extract. Both are available at specialty food stores and some well-stocked grocery stores.

If you have a disher or small ice cream scoop, use it to scoop the cookie dough, packing as you scoop; that way you can avoid the need to squeeze the dough into a ball.

Variation

Try orange or grapefruit zest in place of the lemon zest.

* *Preheat oven to 350°F (180°C)*
* *2 baking sheets, lined with parchment paper*

1 $\frac{1}{2}$ cups	unsalted butter, softened	375 mL
1 cup	granulated sugar	250 mL
1 tbsp	grated lemon zest	15 mL
1 tsp	lemon oil (see Tips, left)	5 mL
3 cups	all-purpose flour	750 mL
1 cup	cake flour	250 mL

1. In work bowl fitted with metal blade, process butter until light and creamy, about 10 seconds. Add sugar, lemon zest and lemon oil and process until incorporated, about 30 seconds. Scrape work bowl to incorporate the whole mixture. Add all-purpose and cake flours and process just until combined, about 10 seconds. If dough is very soft, transfer to a bowl and refrigerate until firm, about 20 minutes.

2. Scoop dough by heaping tablespoonfuls (15 mL) and squeeze into a ball (see Tips, left). Place on prepared baking sheets, about 2 inches (5 cm) apart. Slightly flatten each cookie by pressing down with the palm of your hand or the bottom of a drinking glass. Bake in preheated oven until edges are very light brown, 12 to 18 minutes. Let cool on baking sheets for 10 minutes before transferring to a wire rack to cool completely.

Orange Zest Cookies

**Makes about
48 cookies**

*These are just like the
butter cookies that I
have every time I travel
to Brussels.*

Tips
Store cookies in an
airtight container for up
to 4 days. You can also
freeze them in resealable
plastic bags for up to
1 month.

I like to use a zester
with five holes to create
long strands of zest for
the decorating. Just cut
the strands of zest a few
times so they are not
too long.

● *Preheat oven to 350°F (180°C)*
● *2 baking sheets, lined with parchment paper*

1 ½ cups	unsalted butter, softened	375 mL
1 cup	packed light brown sugar	250 mL
1 tbsp	orange zest, divided (see Tips, left)	15 mL
4 cups	all-purpose flour	1 L

1. In work bowl fitted with metal blade, process butter
   until light and creamy, about 10 seconds. Add brown
   sugar and ½ tbsp (7 mL) of the orange zest and
   process until incorporated, about 30 seconds.
   Scrape work bowl to incorporate the whole mixture.
   Add flour and process just until combined, about
   10 seconds. If dough is very soft, transfer to a bowl
   and refrigerate until firm, about 20 minutes.

2. Scoop dough by heaping tablespoonfuls (15 mL) and
   squeeze into a ball. Place on prepared baking sheets,
   about 2 inches (5 cm) apart. Slightly flatten each
   cookie by pressing down with the palm of your hand
   or the bottom of a drinking glass. Place a small amount
   of the remaining orange zest on each cookie. Bake in
   preheated oven until edges are very light brown, 12 to
   18 minutes. Let cool on baking sheets for 10 minutes
   before transferring to a wire rack to cool completely.

Strawberry Almond Cookies

Makes about 36 cookies

I love how these cookies use dried strawberries, which you can find year round at health food stores and some large supermarkets.

Tips

Store cookies in an airtight container for up to 4 days. You can also freeze them in resealable plastic bags for up to 1 month.

To toast almonds: Place almonds on a baking sheet and toast, stirring partway through, in a preheated 400°F (200°C) oven for 10 minutes. Make sure to toast them for the full 10 minutes to achieve the maximum flavor.

Variation

If dried strawberries are difficult to locate, use dried cranberries, raisins or dried blueberries instead.

- *Preheat oven to 350°F (180°C)*
- *2 baking sheets, lined with parchment paper*

4 oz	dried strawberries	125 g
4 oz	hot water	125 g
1½ cups	unsalted butter, softened	375 mL
1 cup	granulated sugar	250 mL
1 tsp	almond extract	5 mL
4 cups	all-purpose flour	1 L
½ cup	whole unblanched almonds, toasted (see Tips, left)	125 mL

1. In a small bowl, combine dried strawberries and hot water. Let soak until berries are soft, about 10 minutes. Drain and set aside.

2. In work bowl fitted with metal blade, process butter until light and creamy, about 10 seconds. Add sugar and almond extract and process until incorporated, about 30 seconds. Scrape work bowl to incorporate the whole mixture. Add flour and almonds and process just until combined, about 10 seconds. With the motor running, add strawberries through the feed tube and process until chopped and incorporated. If dough is very soft, transfer to a bowl and refrigerate until firm, about 20 minutes.

2. Scoop dough by heaping tablespoonfuls (15 mL) and squeeze into a ball. Place on prepared baking sheets, about 2 inches (5 cm) apart. Slightly flatten each cookie by pressing down with the palm of your hand or the bottom of a drinking glass. Bake in preheated oven until edges are light brown, 12 to 18 minutes. Let cool on baking sheets for 10 minutes before transferring to a wire rack to cool completely.

Pecan Pumpkin Harvest Cookies

Makes about 40 cookies

These cookies have all the flavors of fall with the addition of chocolate, which I love any time of the year.

Tips

Store cookies in an airtight container for up to 4 days. You can also freeze them in resealable plastic bags for up to 1 month.

If you have an extra chocolate bar on hand, chop that up into chunks and use instead of the chocolate chips.

Variation

Try hazelnuts in place of the pecans.

● *Preheat oven to 350°F (180°C)*
● *2 baking sheets, lined with parchment paper*

1 ½ cups	granulated sugar	375 mL
1 cup	Pumpkin Purée (see recipe, page 86) or canned pumpkin purée (not pie filling)	250 mL
½ cup	unsalted butter, softened	125 mL
1	egg	1
1 tsp	vanilla	5 mL
2 ½ cups	all-purpose flour	625 mL
2 tsp	ground cinnamon	10 mL
1 tsp	ground nutmeg	5 mL
1 tsp	baking powder	5 mL
1 tsp	baking soda	5 mL
½ tsp	salt	2 mL
1 cup	semisweet chocolate chips	250 mL
1 cup	chopped and toasted pecans	250 mL

1. In work bowl fitted with metal blade, process sugar, pumpkin, butter, egg and vanilla until light and creamy, about 30 seconds. Scrape work bowl to incorporate the whole mixture. Add flour, cinnamon, nutmeg, baking powder, baking soda and salt and process just until combined, about 10 seconds. Transfer to a large bowl. Fold in chocolate chips and pecans. If dough is very soft, refrigerate until firm, about 20 minutes.

2. Scoop dough by heaping tablespoonfuls (15 mL) and place on prepared baking sheets, about 2 inches (5 cm) apart. Bake in preheated oven until edges are light brown, 12 to 18 minutes. Let cool on baking sheets for 10 minutes before transferring to a wire rack to cool completely.

Oatmeal Cinnamon Raisin Cookies

Makes about 36 cookies

I like how these cookies stay soft and moist even days after baking.

Tips

Store cookies in an airtight container for up to 4 days. You can also freeze them in resealable plastic bags for up to 1 month.

There is no need to soak the raisins if they are soft and fresh.

Variation

Replace raisins with dried cranberries during the holidays for a red festive look to your cookies. Dried cranberries are available at specialty food stores and some large supermarkets.

● *Preheat oven to 350°F (180°C)*
● *2 baking sheets, lined with parchment paper*

1 cup	golden raisins (see Tips, left)	250 mL
1/4 cup	hot water	50 mL
1 cup	unsalted butter, softened	250 mL
3/4 cup	granulated sugar	175 mL
3/4 cup	packed light brown sugar	175 mL
1 tsp	vanilla	5 mL
1	egg	1
3 cups	old-fashioned rolled oats	750 mL
2 cups	all-purpose flour	500 mL
1 tsp	ground cinnamon	5 mL
1/2 tsp	baking soda	2 mL
1/2 tsp	salt	2 mL

1. In a small bowl, combine raisins and hot water. Let soak until raisins are soft, about 10 minutes. Drain. Set aside.

2. In work bowl fitted with metal blade, process butter until light and creamy, about 10 seconds. Add granulated and brown sugars and vanilla. Process until incorporated, about 30 seconds. Add egg and process until incorporated, about 5 seconds. Scrape work bowl to incorporate the whole mixture. Add rolled oats, flour, cinnamon, baking soda and salt and process just until combined, about 10 seconds. With the motor running, add raisins through the feed tube and process until incorporated. If dough is very soft, transfer to a bowl and refrigerate until firm, about 20 minutes.

3. Scoop dough by heaping tablespoonfuls (15 mL) and squeeze into a ball. Place on prepared baking sheets, about 2 inches (5 cm) apart. Slightly flatten each cookie by pressing down with the palm of your hand or the bottom of a drinking glass. Bake in preheated oven until edges are light brown, 12 to 18 minutes. Let cool on baking sheets for 10 minutes before transferring to a wire rack to cool completely.

Peanut Sandwich Cookies

Makes 24 cookies

This is one of my mom's favorite cookies. In fact, anything with peanut butter is a favorite of hers.

Tips

These cookies are best eaten within a few days.

If the filling is too wet, add additional sugar; if too dry, add a few drops of milk.

Variation

I like rolling the edges of the filled cookies in chopped roasted peanuts.

- *Preheat oven to 375°F (190°C)*
- *2 baking sheets, lined with parchment paper*

FILLING

8 oz	cream cheese, softened	250 g
½ cup	confectioner's (icing) sugar	125 mL
¼ cup	creamy peanut butter	50 mL

COOKIE DOUGH

1¾ cups	all-purpose flour	425 mL
1 cup	granulated sugar, divided	250 mL
½ cup	packed light brown sugar	125 mL
½ cup	shortening	125 mL
½ cup	creamy peanut butter	125 mL
1	egg	1
2 tbsp	milk	25 mL
1 tsp	baking soda	5 mL
1 tsp	vanilla	5 mL
½ tsp	salt	2 mL

1. *Filling:* In work bowl fitted with metal blade, process cream cheese, confectioner's sugar and peanut butter until smooth, about 1 minute. Transfer to a small bowl. Set aside.

2. *Cookie Dough:* In clean work bowl fitted with metal blade, process flour, ½ cup (125 mL) of the granulated sugar, brown sugar, shortening, peanut butter, egg, milk, baking soda, vanilla and salt until smooth, about 2 minutes. Transfer to a bowl and refrigerate until firm, about 25 minutes.

3. Shape dough into 48 1-inch (2.5 cm) balls. Roll in remaining granulated sugar. Place on prepared baking sheets, about 2 inches (5 cm) apart. Slightly flatten each cookie by pressing down with the palm of your hand or the bottom of a drinking glass. Bake in preheated oven until edges are light brown, 10 to 14 minutes. Let cool on baking sheets for 20 minutes before transferring to a wire rack to cool completely.

4. Spread half of the cookies with 2 tsp (10 mL) each of the filling. Top with remaining cookies to form sandwiches.

Cinnamon Apple Shortbread

Makes about 36 cookies

Here's a shortbread that has a crisp apple taste in every bite.

Tips

Store cookies in an airtight container for up to 4 days. You can also freeze them in resealable plastic bags for up to 1 month.

The apple needs to be cored and quartered first; otherwise it may just spin around the work bowl.

Variation

Try using a ripe pear in place of the apple.

- *Preheat oven to 350°F (180°C)*
- *2 baking sheets, lined with parchment paper*

1	baking apple, such as Granny Smith, cored, peeled and quartered (see Tips, left)	1
1 cup	unsalted butter, softened	250 mL
¾ cup	granulated sugar	175 mL
1 tbsp	vanilla	15 mL
3¼ cups	all-purpose flour	800 mL
2 tsp	ground cinnamon	10 mL

1. In work bowl fitted with metal blade, pulse apple until finely chopped, about 20 times. Add butter, sugar and vanilla and process until light and creamy, about 10 seconds. Scrape work bowl to incorporate the whole mixture. Add flour and cinnamon and process just until combined, about 10 seconds. If dough is very soft, transfer to a bowl and refrigerate until firm, about 20 minutes.

2. Scoop dough by heaping tablespoonfuls (15 mL) and squeeze into a ball. Place on prepared baking sheets, about 2 inches (5 cm) apart. Slightly flatten each cookie by pressing down with the palm of your hand or the bottom of a drinking glass. Bake in preheated oven until edges are light brown, 12 to 18 minutes. Let cool on baking sheets for 10 minutes before transferring to a wire rack to cool completely.

Fast and Easy Pizza Dough (page 116)
Overleaf: Apple Spice Pie (page 136)

Sugar and Spice Cookies

These cookies are great with strong coffee on a cold, snowy day.

Tips

Store cookies in an airtight container for up to 4 days. You can also freeze them in resealable plastic bags for up to 1 month.

If your brown sugar is hard, soften it in the microwave on High for 10 to 20 seconds.

Variations

Instead of cinnamon, nutmeg, cloves, cardamom and mace use 2¼ tsp (11 mL) pumpkin pie spice.

- *Preheat oven to 350°F (180°C)*
- *2 baking sheets, lined with parchment paper*

1 cup	unsalted butter, softened	250 mL
¾ cup	packed light brown sugar	175 mL
1 tbsp	vanilla	15 mL
3 cups	all-purpose flour	750 mL
1 tsp	ground cinnamon	5 mL
½ tsp	ground nutmeg	2 mL
¼ tsp	ground cloves	1 mL
¼ tsp	ground cardamom	1 mL
¼ tsp	ground mace	1 mL

1. In work bowl fitted with metal blade, process butter until light and creamy, about 10 seconds. Add brown sugar and vanilla and process until incorporated, about 30 seconds. Scrape work bowl to incorporate the whole mixture. Add flour, cinnamon, nutmeg, cloves, cardamom and mace and process just until combined, about 10 seconds. If dough is very soft, transfer to a bowl and refrigerate until firm, about 20 minutes.

2. Scoop dough by heaping tablespoonfuls (15 mL) and squeeze into a ball. Place on prepared baking sheets, about 2 inches (5 cm) apart. Slightly flatten each cookie by pressing down with the palm of your hand or the bottom of a drinking glass. Bake in preheated oven until edges are light brown, 12 to 18 minutes. Let cool on baking sheets for 10 minutes before transferring to a wire rack to cool completely.

Quadruple Chocolate Chunk Cookies (page 130)

Quadruple Chocolate Chunk Cookies

My best cookie ever! I make this cookie in every cooking school where I teach. Just the title alone excites the class.

Tips

Store cookies in an airtight container for up to 4 days. You can also freeze them in resealable plastic bags for up to 1 month.

Purchase new baking soda when you haven't baked for a few months. Do not use soda kept in the refrigerator or freezer as a deodorizer because it may take on the taste of fish or other items.

Variations

Try some of the mint or peanut butter chips in place of the other varieties in this recipe.

For larger cookies, scoop by level ¼ cup (50 mL) to yield 32 cookies.

- *Preheat oven to 350°F (180°C)*
- *2 baking sheets, lined with parchment paper*

2 cups	granulated sugar	500 mL
1¼ cups	unsalted butter, softened	300 mL
2	eggs	2
2 tsp	vanilla	10 mL
3 cups	all-purpose flour	750 mL
¾ cup	unsweetened Dutch-process cocoa powder, sifted	175 mL
1 tsp	baking soda	5 mL
½ tsp	salt	2 mL
2 cups	white chocolate chips	500 mL
1 cup	semisweet chocolate chips	250 mL
1 cup	milk chocolate chips	250 mL

1. In work bowl fitted with metal blade, process sugar and butter until creamy, about 10 seconds. With the motor running, add eggs and vanilla through the feed tube and process until incorporated. Scrape work bowl to incorporate the whole mixture. Add flour, cocoa powder, baking soda and salt and process just until combined, about 1 minute. Transfer to a large bowl. Add white, semisweet and milk chocolate chips. If dough is very soft, refrigerate until firm, about 20 minutes.

2. Scoop dough by heaping tablespoonfuls (15 mL) and squeeze into a ball. Place on prepared baking sheets, about 2 inches (5 cm) apart. Slightly flatten each cookie by pressing down with the palm of your hand or the bottom of a drinking glass. Bake in preheated oven until edges are firm, 12 to 18 minutes. Let cool on baking sheets for 10 minutes before transferring to a wire rack to cool completely.

The Perfect Fudgey Brownie

Makes 24 brownies

This brownie is so rich and fast to prepare that it deserves its name — it is the perfect brownie.

Tips

Store brownies wrapped in plastic wrap for up to 5 days. You can also freeze them wrapped in foil for up to 1 month.

Make sure the chocolate is cool to the touch prior to adding it to the other ingredients.

Variation

After the brownies are baked and still hot, brush the top with ¼ cup (50 mL) coffee-flavored liqueur for an adult brownie.

- *Preheat oven to 350°F (180°C)*
- *13-by 9-inch (3 L) metal baking pan, lined with foil and sprayed with nonstick spray or parchment paper*

1½ lbs	semisweet chocolate, chopped	750 g
1½ cups	almonds	375 mL
½ cup	all-purpose flour	125 mL
2 cups	Traditional Mayonnaise (see recipe, page 36) or store-bought	500 mL
8	eggs	8
1½ cups	granulated sugar	375 mL
6 oz	milk chocolate, cut into chunks	175 g
¼ cup	confectioner's (icing) sugar	50 mL

1. In a double boiler over hot, not boiling water, melt semisweet chocolate. Set aside and let cool slightly.

2. In work bowl fitted with metal blade, process almonds and flour until very finely ground, about 1 minute. Add mayonnaise, eggs, sugar and melted chocolate and process until well blended, about 1 minute. Fold milk chocolate chunks into batter.

3. Spread mixture into prepared pan. Bake in preheated oven until a toothpick inserted into center comes out with loose crumbs and top is firm, 30 to 35 minutes. Let cool on a wire rack. Sprinkle with confectioner's sugar. Cut into squares.

Chocolate Raspberry Brownies

Makes 24 brownies

Raspberries are the perfect fruit to accompany this rich chocolate brownie.

Tips

Store brownies wrapped in plastic wrap for up to 5 days. You can also freeze them wrapped in foil for up to 1 month.

If the raspberries are large, cut them into smaller pieces.

Variation

You can use 1 cup (250 mL) seedless raspberry preserves in place of the raspberries.

- *Preheat oven to 350°F (180°C)*
- *13-by 9-inch (3 L) metal baking pan, lined with foil and sprayed with nonstick spray or parchment paper*

1 1/4 cups	granulated sugar	300 mL
3/4 cup	unsalted butter, melted	175 mL
2	eggs	2
1 tsp	vanilla	5 mL
1 1/2 cups	all-purpose flour	375 mL
1/2 cup	unsweetened Dutch-process cocoa powder, sifted	125 mL
1 tsp	baking powder	5 mL
1/4 tsp	baking soda	1 mL
1 cup	milk, at room temperature	250 mL
1 cup	fresh or frozen raspberries, thawed and drained if frozen	250 mL
	Bittersweet Fudge Frosting (optional) (see recipe, page 172)	

1. In work bowl fitted with metal blade, process sugar, butter, eggs and vanilla until combined, about 20 seconds. Add flour, cocoa powder, baking powder and baking soda and process until it begins to gather, 20 to 30 seconds. With the motor running, add milk in a steady stream through the feed tube until incorporated.

2. Transfer mixture to a bowl and carefully fold in raspberries. Transfer to prepared baking pan. Bake in preheated oven until a toothpick inserted into the center comes out with loose crumbs and top is firm, 25 to 35 minutes. Let cool on a wire rack before cutting into squares.

3. Frost with Bittersweet Fudge Frosting, if desired.

Pies, Tarts and Pastries

All-Butter Pie Pastry 134

Spiced Pastry 135

Apple Spice Pie 136

Berry Pie 137

Pumpkin Pecan Pie 138

Buttery Tart Pastry 139

Chocolate Tart Pastry 140

Pear Almond Cream Tarts 141

Caramel Chocolate Tarts 142

Apple Pockets 144

Pear Pandowdy 146

Apple Crisp with Crumb Topping 148

All-Butter Pie Pastry

In less then 5 minutes you can have a flaky pie crust without all of the fuss of hand mixing.

Tips
To roll out dough: Place the chilled disk of dough on a flat surface lightly dusted with flour. Using a rolling pin, start at the center of the dough roll out toward the edge of the circle, picking up the pin between rolling and placing it back in the center. Continue to roll out in every direction (like the points on a compass) to keep dough in a circle, to the desired thickness and size. Keep the rolling surface lightly dusted with flour as you roll. In general, roll out until the circle of dough is about 2 inches (5 cm) larger than the inverted pie plate.

If your dough forms a ball in the work bowl, it may be too tough. To save the dough, turn the machine off and sprinkle dough with ¼ cup (50 mL) all-purpose flour. Pulse 5 times, then proceed with Step 2.

1⅔ cups	cake flour	400 mL
1 cup	all-purpose flour	250 mL
1 tbsp	granulated sugar	15 mL
1 tsp	salt	5 mL
¾ cup	cold unsalted butter, cut into small chunks	175 mL
3 to 6 tbsp ice water (approx.)		45 to 60 mL

1. In work bowl fitted with metal blade, process cake and all-purpose flours, sugar and salt until combined, about 10 seconds. Remove lid and distribute butter evenly over top. Cover and pulse until mixture resembles coarse crumbs, about 20 times. Place water in a container with a pouring spout and, with the motor running, slowly pour through the feed tube in a steady stream just until dough begins to gather. You may not use all the water, which is fine.

2. Turn out dough onto a clean surface and gather into a ball. Press the ball down and wrap in plastic wrap. Refrigerate until firm enough to roll out for your pie, 10 to 20 minutes. (For rolling instructions, see Tips, left)

Spiced Pastry

Years ago, I created this crust for a story I wrote for my hometown newspaper. It still runs every holiday season.

Tips

Freeze dough in an airtight container for up to 1 month.

If your dough forms a ball in the work bowl, it may be too tough. To save the dough, turn the machine off and sprinkle dough with ¼ cup (50 mL) all-purpose flour. Pulse 5 times, then proceed with Step 2.

Variation

Try using ½ tsp (2 mL) ground cloves or mace in place of the nutmeg.

1½ cups	cake flour	375 mL
1½ cups	all-purpose flour	375 mL
2 tsp	ground cinnamon	10 mL
2 tsp	granulated sugar	10 mL
1 tsp	freshly ground nutmeg	5 mL
½ tsp	salt	2 mL
1 cup	cold unsalted butter, cut into small chunks	250 mL
½ cup	ice water	125 mL

1. In work bowl fitted with metal blade, process cake and all-purpose flours, cinnamon, sugar, nutmeg and salt until combined, about 10 seconds. Remove lid and distribute butter evenly over top. Cover and pulse until mixture resembles coarse crumbs, about 10 times. Place water in a container with a pouring spout and, with the motor running, slowly pour in a steady stream through the feed tube until dough begins to gather. You may not use all the water, which is fine.

2. Turn out dough onto a clean surface and form into 2 disks. Press disks down and wrap in plastic wrap. Refrigerate until firm enough to roll out for your pie, 10 to 20 minutes. (To roll out dough, see Tips, page 134.)

Apple Spice Pie

You can create this pie faster than going to the store or bakery and purchasing one.

Tip

I like to use 3 different types of baking apples in my pie. Good baking apples are McIntosh, Jonagold, Granny Smith and Pippin.

- *Preheat oven to 400°F (200°C)*
- *9-inch (23 cm) pie plate*

1	recipe Spiced Pastry (see recipe, page 135)	1
6	large baking apples, peeled, cored and quartered (see Tip, left)	6
¼ cup	freshly squeezed lemon juice	50 mL
1 cup	granulated sugar	250 mL
3 tbsp	all-purpose flour	45 mL
1½ tsp	ground cinnamon	7 mL
½ tsp	freshly ground nutmeg	2 mL
2 tbsp	unsalted butter, melted	25 mL
2 tsp	water	10 mL
2 tsp	coarse sugar	10 mL

1. On a lightly floured surface, roll out half of the pastry to fit the bottom of a 9-inch (23 cm) pie plate. Roll the remaining half into a ¼-inch (0.5 cm) thick circle for the top. Set aside. (To roll out dough, see Tips, page 134.)

2. In work bowl fitted with slicing blade and with the motor running, slice apples. Transfer to a bowl filled with enough water to cover apple slices and lemon juice. Set aside.

3. In a large bowl, blend together sugar, flour, cinnamon and nutmeg until fully incorporated. Drain apples and add to sugar mixture. Toss to fully coat apple slices. Fill bottom crust with apple mixture. Drizzle butter over top. Place top pastry crust over filling. Seal and crimp edges, trimming off any excess dough. Using a knife, make several slits in the top of the dough, or use a small cookie cutter to cut a design from the center of the pie for steam to escape. Brush top with water and sprinkle with coarse sugar. Bake in preheated oven until light brown and sugar has caramelized slightly, 40 to 55 minutes. Let cool for 1 hour before cutting.

Berry Pie

Serves 8

You can make this pie with frozen berries. Your family will think you used fresh!

Tips

If using fresh berries, mix a combination of blackberries, raspberries and strawberries.

Once thawed, the berries will yield about 4 cups (1 L). Include any juices that accumulate as berries thaw.

• *Preheat oven to 425°F (220°C)*
• *10-inch (25 cm) deep dish pie plate*

1	recipe All-Butter Pie Pastry (see recipe, page 134)	1
2	packages (each 16 oz/454 g) frozen mixed berries (about 8 cups/2 L), thawed	2
1½ cups	granulated sugar	375 mL
½ cup	cornstarch	125 mL
2 tsp	freshly squeezed lemon juice	10 mL
¼ tsp	salt	1 mL

1. On a lightly floured surface, roll out half of the pastry to fit the bottom of a 10-inch (25 cm) pie plate. Set aside. (To roll out dough, see Tips, page 134).

2. Place half of the berries in a large bowl. Chop any of the larger strawberries. Set aside. In work bowl fitted with metal blade, process remaining berries, sugar, cornstarch, lemon juice and salt until smooth, about 30 seconds. Stir into bowl with whole berries.

3. Fill bottom crust with berry mixture. Roll the remaining half of pastry into a ¼-inch (0.5 cm) thick circle for the top. Using a cooking cutter or the tip of a sharp knife, cut out three 1-inch (2.5 cm) holes in the center of the pastry, leaving about ¼-inch (0.5 cm) between holes. Position the top pastry crust over filling so the holes are in the center. Trim off all but 1-inch (2.5 cm) of excess dough. Fold top edge over bottom pastry to seal and crimp edges. Using a knife, make several slits in the top of the dough for steam to escape.

4. Bake in preheated oven for 20 minutes. Reduce temperature to 375°F (190°C) and bake until the top is light brown and the berries are bubbling, about 45 minutes. Let cool completely on a wire rack prior to cutting.

Pumpkin Pecan Pie

Serves 8

I love making both pumpkin and pecan pies. Here they are together in one pie.

Tip

Check your pie at 40 minutes. If a knife comes out runny with a little bit of firm pieces attached, the pie needs 10 minutes more; if you see only firm pieces but the knife is still not clean, it needs 5 additional minutes. You never want the knife to come out completely clean the first time because it might be overbaked at this point.

Variation

Reduce milk by ¼ cup (50 mL) and use coffee-flavored liqueur instead.

- *Preheat oven to 375°F (190°C)*
- *9-inch (23 cm) pie plate*

½	recipe Spiced Pastry (see recipe, page 135)	½
½ cup	pecans halves	125 mL
1½ cups	Pumpkin Purée (see recipe, page 86) or canned pumpkin purée (not pie filling)	375 mL
¾ cup	packed light brown sugar	175 mL
2 tsp	ground cinnamon	10 mL
1 tsp	ground ginger	5 mL
½ tsp	ground cloves	2 mL
½ tsp	salt	2 mL
½ tsp	freshly ground nutmeg	2 mL
3	eggs	3
1¼ cups	milk	300 mL
¾ cup	evaporated milk	175 mL

1. On a lightly floured surface, roll out pastry to fit the bottom of a 9-inch (23 cm) pie plate. (To roll out dough, see Tips, page 134).

2. In work bowl fitted with metal blade, pulse pecans until finely chopped, about 15 times. Do not overprocess or you will get pecan butter. Spread pecans over pastry.

3. In same work bowl fitted with metal blade, process pumpkin, brown sugar, cinnamon, ginger, cloves, salt and nutmeg until smooth, about 30 seconds. With the motor running, add eggs through the feed tube. Then pour in milk and evaporated milk in a steady stream and process until incorporated. Pour mixture over pecans in prepared pie shell. Bake in preheated oven until crust is firm and light brown and a knife inserted into the center of filling comes out clean, 40 to 50 minutes (see Tip, left).

Buttery Tart Pastry

Makes 2 tart shells

A tart crust, unlike a pie crust, needs to be able to stand on its own outside of a pan. This rich and buttery crust will enhance your tart pastries.

Tips

Freeze unbaked dough in an airtight container in the freezer for up to 1 month.

You can also use this dough for small individual tart shells. It makes twelve 3-inch (7.5 cm) tarts.

Variation

Savory Buttery Tart Pastry: You can make a savory tart shell by omitting the sugar and adding ¼ cup (50 mL) additional all-purpose flour.

● *Two 8-inch (20 cm) metal tart pans with removable bottoms*

2½ cups	all-purpose flour	625 mL
¼ cup	granulated sugar	50 mL
½ tsp	salt	2 mL
1 cup	cold unsalted butter, cut into chunks	250 mL
2	egg yolks	2
3 tbsp	cold water	45 mL

1. In work bowl fitted with metal blade, pulse flour, sugar and salt until combined, about 5 times. Remove lid and distribute butter evenly over top. Cover and pulse until mixture resembles coarse crumbs, about 20 times.

2. In a container with a pouring spout, mix together egg yolks and cold water. With the motor running, slowly pour mixture through the feed tube in a steady stream until dough begins to gather. Do not overprocess or let a ball form. The dough will be somewhat crumbly at this point. Transfer dough to a board and press lightly with palm of your hand to warm up. It is now ready to press out into tart pans.

3. Press half of the dough evenly into sides and bottoms of each pan. Trim excess dough from top.

Chocolate Tart Pastry

Makes 2 tart shells

A dark rich chocolate tart crust looks fantastic with a caramel filling (see Caramel Chocolate Tarts, page 142).

Tips

Freeze unbaked dough in an airtight container in the freezer for up to 1 month.

I don't use pie weights when blind baking tart shells. I check the tart partway through the baking and then press any bloating down with a fork or scrunched up paper towel.

Variation

Try adding 1 tsp (5 mL) ground cinnamon in the dough if you are making something that cinnamon will enhance.

● *Two 8-inch (20 cm) metal tart pans with removable bottoms*

2 cups	all-purpose flour	500 mL
½ cup	unsweetened Dutch-process cocoa powder	125 mL
½ cup	granulated sugar	125 mL
½ tsp	salt	2 mL
1 cup	cold unsalted butter, cut into chunks	250 mL
2	egg yolks	2
¼ cup	cold water	50 mL

1. In work bowl fitted with metal blade, pulse flour, cocoa powder, sugar and salt until combined, about 5 times. Remove lid and distribute butter evenly over top. Cover and pulse until mixture resembles coarse crumbs, about 20 times.

2. In a container with a pouring spout, mix together egg yolks and cold water. With the motor running, slowly pour mixture through the feed tube in a steady stream until dough begins to gather. Do not overprocess or let a ball form. The dough will be somewhat crumbly at this point. Place the dough on a board and press lightly with palm of your hand to warm up, if necessary.

3. Press half of the dough evenly into sides and bottoms of each pan. Trim excess dough from top.

4. To bake with filling: Fill crust with your favorite filling and follow recipe directions. To bake unfilled: Prick bottom and sides of crust. Bake in preheated 425°F (220°C) oven until dry looking, 18 to 22 minutes. Let cool completely. Fill with desired filling, such as caramel chocolate (page 142).

Pear Almond Cream Tarts

Makes 2 tarts

These are the beautiful tarts that you see in French pastry shop windows. I'm always amazed at how expensive they are when they're so simple to make.

Tip
You can make the cream a few days prior to use. Cover and refrigerate and then stir before using.

Variation

Try using 6 fresh peaches, cut in half, or ½ cup (125 mL) canned peaches or cherries, drained, in place of the pears.

- *Preheat oven to 375°F (190°C)*

I	recipe Buttery Tart Pastry (see recipe, page 139)	I
7 oz	almond paste	210 g
¾ cup	granulated sugar	175 mL
⅓ cup	unsalted butter, softened	75 mL
3	eggs	3
I tsp	vanilla	5 mL
¾ cup	cake flour	175 mL
12	large canned pear halves, drained	12

1. Set aside prepared tart shells until filling is ready.

2. In work bowl fitted with metal blade, process almond paste and sugar until softened, about 30 seconds. Add butter and process until incorporated. With the motor running, add eggs and vanilla through the feed tube until well incorporated, about 20 seconds. Add flour and process until smooth, about 30 seconds.

3. Divide mixture evenly between tart shells. Slice each pear half vertically into about 8 slices, trying to keep the pear looking like it's still intact. Place sliced pear over almond cream, pressing to fan pear. Do this 5 more times around the tart so you have 6 pear halves on each tart. Bake in preheated oven until crust is light brown and filling is set, about 45 to 60 minutes.

Caramel Chocolate Tarts

Makes 2 tarts

This chocolate-rich tart is filled with a sweet caramel chocolate cream.

Tip

Make sure the chocolate is cool prior to adding it to the milk or it may turn into chocolate chips.

Variation

Add $\frac{1}{2}$ cup (125 mL) hazelnuts to the mixture for a nutty taste.

● *Instant-read thermometer*

1	recipe Chocolate Tart Pastry (see recipe, page 140), baked	1
4 oz	unsweetened chocolate, chopped	125 g
1 cup	granulated sugar	250 mL
$\frac{1}{3}$ cup	all-purpose flour	75 mL
1 tbsp	cornstarch	15 mL
1 tsp	instant coffee granules	5 mL
Pinch	salt	Pinch
4 oz	soft caramels, cut into small pieces (about 12)	125 g
2 cups	milk	500 mL
5	egg yolks, beaten	5
1 tsp	vanilla	5 mL
	Whipped cream	

1. Set aside prepared baked tart shells until filling is ready.

2. In a microwave-safe bowl, microwave chocolate on Medium, stirring every 30 seconds, until soft and almost melted, 1 to $1\frac{1}{2}$ minutes. Stir until completely melted and smooth. Let cool slightly.

3. Meanwhile, in work bowl fitted with metal blade, process sugar, flour, cornstarch, coffee granules and salt until combined, about 10 seconds. Add caramels to work bowl. Set aside.

4. In a saucepan over medium heat, bring milk, chocolate and eggs yolks to a simmer, stirring, until an instant-read thermometer registers 160°F (71°C) and mixture is thick enough to coat the back of a spoon. Add vanilla. With the motor running, add to sugar mixture through the feed tube until blended and caramels are chopped.

5. Divide mixture evenly between tart shells. Refrigerate, covered, until set, at least 1 to 2 hours or for up to 4 hours. Serve with whipped cream.

Apple Pockets

Makes 18 pockets

I like to keep these on hand in the freezer in case of company.

Tips

If you have a smaller package of puff pastry, the pastry may be thinner but will still work.

You can freeze the apple pockets for up to 1 month. Cover with foil and reheat in a preheated 350°F (180°C) oven for 10 minutes.

Variation

You can use a combination of apples and pears.

● *Preheat oven to 425°F (220°C)*
● *Baking sheet, lined with parchment paper*

3	large baking apples (about 1½ lbs/750 g) (see Tip, page 136)	3
2 tbsp	freshly squeezed lemon juice	25 mL
½ cup	lightly packed brown sugar	125 mL
1½ tbsp	all-purpose flour	22 mL
1 tsp	ground cinnamon	5 mL
½ tsp	freshly ground nutmeg	2 mL
1	package (18 oz/540 g) puff pastry, thawed (see Tips, left)	1
2 tsp	water	10 mL
2 tsp	coarse sugar	10 mL

1. Peel, quarter and core apples. In work bowl fitted with slicing blade, slice apples. Transfer to a large bowl filled with enough water to cover apple slices and lemon juice. Set aside.

2. In another large bowl, blend together brown sugar, flour, cinnamon and nutmeg. Drain apples well and add to sugar mixture. Toss to fully coat apple pieces. Set aside.

3. Working with one half of pastry, on a lightly floured board, roll one sheet of pastry into a 12-inch (30 cm) square. Using a pizza cutter, cut equally, horizontally and vertically, so you end up with 3 strips by 3 strips to make 9 squares.

4. Place about $\frac{1}{4}$ cup (50 mL) of the sliced apple mixture into center of each square of pastry. Working with one square at a time, starting with two opposite corners, fold into the center and press to seal over the apple filling. Repeat with third and fourth corners, meeting over top first ones to resemble an envelope and press to seal edges. If pastry seems dry, lightly brush edges with water before folding to ensure a good seal. Transfer to prepared baking sheet, about 2 inches (5 cm) apart. Brush each with a little water and sprinkle with coarse sugar. Repeat with remaining pastry and filling to make 18 pockets. Bake in preheated oven until golden brown and puffed up, 18 to 24 minutes. Serve hot.

Pear Pandowdy

A pandowdy is an old-fashioned dessert often made with apples. Here I've used pears. The dough is placed on top of the fruit prior to baking to form a crisp crumbly topping. Serve warm with vanilla ice cream, if desired.

Tip

Pears do not have to be peeled, just core and process.

Variation

You can use baking apples, such as McIntosh, Jonagold or Pippin, in place of the pears.

● *Preheat oven to 375°F (190°C)*
● *13-by 9-inch (3 L) baking dish, buttered*

TOPPING

¾ cup	cake flour	175 mL
¾ cup	all-purpose flour	175 mL
2 tsp	granulated sugar	10 mL
¼ tsp	salt	1 mL
½ cup	cold unsalted butter, cut into chunks	125 mL
¼ cup	cold water	50 mL

FILLING

1 cup	granulated sugar	250 mL
3 tbsp	all-purpose flour	45 mL
1½ tsp	ground cinnamon	7 mL
½ tsp	freshly ground nutmeg	2 mL
8	pears, cored and quartered, such as Anjou or Bartlett (see Tip, left)	8
2 tbsp	unsalted butter, melted	25 mL
2 tbsp	apple cider or apple juice	25 mL

1. *Topping:* In work bowl fitted with metal blade, process cake and all-purpose flours, sugar and salt until combined, about 5 seconds. Remove lid and distribute butter evenly over top. Cover and pulse until mixture resembles coarse crumbs, about 20 times. The mixture should be in small pieces. With the motor running, add water through the feed tube until dough begins to gather. Remove dough and pat into a ball. If it is sticky at this point you can cover and place in the refrigerator until firm, 5 to 10 minutes. Roll out to 13-by 9-inch (32.5 by 23 cm) rectangle, ¼-inch (0.5 cm) thick. Cut into squares. Set aside.

2. *Filling:* In a large bowl, blend together sugar, flour, cinnamon and nutmeg. Set aside.

3. Replace metal blade with slicing blade and slice pears. Add pears to sugar mixture and toss to fully coat. Transfer to prepared baking dish. Slowly drizzle butter and apple cider over top. Place dough squares over top. Bake in preheated oven until pears are tender and top is golden brown, 45 to 55 minutes.

Apple Crisp with Crumb Topping

Serves 16

In grade school I would swap anything for the cafeteria's signature apple crisp. This fruity dessert takes me back to those '70s years.

Tip

Make sure the butter is cold from the refrigerator or topping will not be crumbly.

Variation

You can add ¼ cup (50 mL) nuts to the topping when processing flour mixture.

- *Preheat oven to 350°F (180°C)*
- *13-by 9-inch (3 L) baking dish, buttered*

TOPPING

1½ cups	all-purpose flour	375 mL
½ cup	lightly packed light brown sugar	125 mL
2 tbsp	granulated sugar	25 mL
½ tsp	ground cinnamon	2 mL
¼ tsp	salt	1 mL
½ cup	cold unsalted butter, cut into chunks	125 mL

FILLING

6	large baking apples, peeled, cored and quartered (see Tip, page 136)	6
1 cup	granulated sugar	250 mL
2 tbsp	all-purpose flour	25 mL
1 tsp	ground cinnamon	5 mL
½ tsp	freshly ground nutmeg	2 mL
¼ tsp	ground cloves	1 mL

1. *Topping:* In work bowl fitted with metal blade, pulse flour, brown and granulated sugars, cinnamon and salt until combined, about 5 times. Remove lid and distribute butter evenly over top. Cover and pulse until mixture resembles coarse crumbs, about 20 times. Transfer to a bowl. Set aside.

2. *Filling:* Replace metal blade with slicing blade and slice apples. In a large bowl, combine sugar, flour, cinnamon, nutmeg and cloves. Add sliced apples and toss to fully coat. Transfer to prepared baking dish. Crumble topping over top. Bake in preheated oven until brown and bubbling, 35 to 40 minutes. Serve warm.

Cakes and Quick Breads

Lemon Mist Cheesecake 150

Citrus Bliss Cheesecake 151

Three-Nut Cheesecake 152

Deep Dark Chocolate Fudge Cheesecake 154

Chocolate Cherry Loaf 156

Banana Pineapple Cake 157

24 Carrot Cake. 158

White Cake 160

Cinnamon Pecan Cupcakes 161

Blueberry Pecan Muffins. 162

Honey Apple Spice Muffins 163

Chocolate Chunk Muffins. 164

Pumpkin Muffins 165

Fresh Savory Herb Scones. 166

Peach Scones. 167

Almond Poppy Seed Scones 168

Chocolate Chip Scones 169

Cream Cheese Icing 170

Buttercream Frosting 171

Bittersweet Fudge Frosting 172

Lemon Mist Cheesecake

Tart yet tangy, lemon cheesecake is refreshing with iced tea on a lazy afternoon.

Tip

To make the lemons easier to juice, roll them firmly on your counter to break up the membranes of the fruit.

Variation

Add ½ tsp (2 mL) grated lemon zest to a graham cracker crust if you can't find lemon cookies.

- *Preheat oven to 325°F (160°C)*
- *9-inch (23 cm) cheesecake pan, or springform pan with 3-inch (7.5 cm) sides, lined with parchment paper*

CRUST

14	lemon cookies (about 6 oz/175 g)	14
¼ cup	unsalted butter, melted	50 mL

FILLING

4	packages (each 8 oz/250 g) cream cheese, softened	4
1 cup	granulated sugar	250 mL
3	eggs	3
2 tbsp	grated lemon zest	25 mL
¼ cup	freshly squeezed lemon juice	50 mL
1 tsp	vanilla	5 mL

1. *Crust:* In work bowl fitted with metal blade, process cookies until finely ground. You should have 1½ cups (375 mL). Transfer to a bowl and mix in butter. Press into bottom of cheesecake pan and freeze until filling is ready.

2. *Filling:* In clean work bowl fitted with metal blade, process cream cheese and sugar until smooth, about 20 seconds. With the motor running, add eggs, lemon zest, lemon juice and vanilla through the feed tube and process until blended. Pour batter over frozen crust, smoothing out to sides of pan.

3. Bake in preheated oven until it starts to pull away from sides of pan but is still a bit loose in center and looks puffy, 45 to 55 minutes. Let cool in pan on a wire rack for 2 hours. Cover with plastic wrap and refrigerate for at least 2 hours before serving.

Citrus Bliss Cheesecake

Tangy orange and lemon flavors come together in one sublime cheesecake.

Tip

The orange juice concentrate packs a powerful orange flavor while the orange juice alone does not.

Variation

Add 1 tsp (5 mL) ground cinnamon for a spiced cheesecake.

- *Preheat oven to 325°F (160°C)*
- *9-inch (23 cm) cheesecake pan, or springform pan with 3-inch (7.5 cm) sides, lined with parchment paper*

CRUST

14	butter cookies (6 oz/175 g)	14
¼ cup	butter, melted	50 mL

FILLING

3	packages (each 8 oz/250 g) cream cheese, softened	3
1 cup	sour cream	250 mL
1 cup	granulated sugar	250 mL
4	eggs	4
1 tbsp	grated lemon zest	15 mL
1 tbsp	grated orange zest	15 mL
2 tbsp	freshly squeezed lemon juice	25 mL
2 tbsp	orange juice concentrate (see Tip, left)	25 mL
2 tsp	vanilla	10 mL

1. *Crust:* In work bowl fitted with metal blade, process cookies until finely ground, about 20 seconds. You should have 1½ cups (375 mL). Transfer to a bowl and mix in butter. Press into bottom of cheesecake pan and freeze until filling is ready.

2. *Filling:* In clean work bowl fitted with metal blade, process cream cheese, sour cream and sugar until smooth, about 20 seconds. With the motor running, add eggs, lemon and orange zests, lemon juice, orange juice concentrate and vanilla through the feed tube and process until blended. Pour batter over frozen crust, smoothing out to sides of pan.

3. Bake in preheated oven until it starts to pull away from sides of pan but is still a bit loose in center and looks puffy, 45 to 55 minutes. Let cool on a wire rack for 2 hours. Cover with plastic wrap and refrigerate for at least 2 hours before serving.

Three-Nut Cheesecake

Serves 10 to 12

A rich nutty taste permeates this creamy cheesecake.

Tip
If you process nuts alone you may get nut butter; adding a little flour to the nuts prevents this by drying the oils.

● *Preheat oven to 350°F (180°C)*
● *9-inch (23 cm) cheesecake pan, or springform pan with 3-inch (7.5 cm) sides, lined with parchment paper*

CRUST

1½ cups	pecans halves	375 mL
¼ cup	all-purpose flour	50 mL
¼ cup	unsalted butter, melted	50 mL

FILLING

1 cup	walnuts halves	250 mL
¾ cup	cashews, unsalted	175 mL
2 tsp	all-purpose flour	10 mL
4	packages (each 8 oz/250 g) cream cheese, softened	4
1⅓ cups	granulated sugar	325 mL
4	eggs	4
1 tbsp	grated lemon zest	15 mL
2 tbsp	freshly squeezed lemon juice	25 mL
1 tsp	vanilla	5 mL
¼ tsp	maple flavoring	1 mL

1. *Crust:* In work bowl fitted with metal blade, process pecans and flour until finely ground, about 20 seconds. Transfer to a bowl and mix in butter. Press into bottom of cheesecake pan. Bake in preheated oven until nuts are toasted, about 10 minutes.

2. *Filling:* In work bowl fitted with metal blade, pulse walnuts, cashews and flour until coarsely chopped, about 15 times. Transfer to a bowl. Set aside.

3. In same work bowl fitted with metal blade, process cream cheese and sugar until smooth, about 20 seconds. With the motor running, add eggs, lemon zest and juice, vanilla and maple flavoring through the feed tube and process until blended. Pour half of the batter over crust, smoothing out to sides of pan. Sprinkle half of the chopped nuts over top. Spoon remaining batter over nuts. Sprinkle remaining nuts over top.

4. Bake in preheated oven until it starts to pull away from sides of pan but is still a bit loose in center and looks puffy, 45 to 55 minutes. Let cool in pan on a wire rack for 2 hours. Cover with plastic wrap and refrigerate for at least 2 hours before serving.

Deep Dark Chocolate Fudge Cheesecake

Here's a chocolate fudge cheesecake that's so rich you'll need a glass of milk to wash it down!

Tip

Make sure the chocolate is cooled to room temperature; otherwise you'll get strange chunks in your batter.

Variation

Use white chips in place of the semisweet for a black and white cheesecake.

● *Preheat oven to 325°F (160°C)*
● *6-inch (15 cm) cheesecake pan, or springform pan with 3-inch (7.5 cm) sides, lined with parchment paper*

CRUST

7	chocolate sandwich cookies (about 3 oz/90 g)	7
2 tbsp	unsalted butter, melted	25 mL

FILLING

4 oz	unsweetened chocolate, melted and cooled	125 g
2	packages (each 8 oz/250 g) cream cheese, softened	2
¾ cup	granulated sugar	175 mL
2	eggs	2
1 tsp	vanilla	5 mL
¼ cup	semisweet chocolate chips	50 mL

1. *Crust:* In work bowl fitted with metal blade, process cookies until finely ground, about 20 seconds. You should have ¾ cup (175 mL). Transfer to a bowl and mix in butter. Press into bottom of cheesecake pan and freeze until filling is ready.

2. *Filling:* In a microwave-safe bowl, microwave chocolate on Medium, stirring every 30 seconds, until soft and almost melted, 1 to 1½ minutes. Stir until completely melted and smooth. Let cool slightly.

3. In clean work bowl fitted with metal blade, process cream cheese and sugar until smooth, about 20 seconds. With the motor running, add melted chocolate, eggs and vanilla through the feed tube and process until blended. Pour batter over crust, smoothing out to sides of pan. Sprinkle chocolate chips over top.

4. Bake in preheated oven until it starts to pull away from sides of pan but is still a bit loose in center and looks puffy, 35 to 45 minutes. Cool on a wire rack for 2 hours. Cover with plastic wrap and refrigerate for at least 2 hours before serving.

Chocolate Cherry Loaf

This rich and flavorful fruitcake is unlike fruitcakes purchased at the store, which are more handy as doorstops than cakes. You'll need a week of preplanning to soak the cherries in brandy but the wait will be worth it.

Tips

If you soak the cherries for longer than 1 week you may have to replace some of the brandy, which will have evaporated.

If you can only find cherries in a 14-oz (398 mL) can, don't worry, it will be enough.

Variation

You can use candied citron or candied pineapple in place of cherries. They should also be soaked in the brandy.

● *9-by 5-inch (2 L) loaf pan, sprayed with nonstick spray*

I	can (15 oz/425 g) cherries in heavy syrup, drained	I
⅔ cup	brandy	150 mL
3 tbsp	lightly packed brown sugar	45 mL
2 tbsp	unsalted butter, softened	25 mL
I tbsp	granulated sugar	15 mL
Pinch	salt	Pinch
I	egg	I
I tbsp	liquid honey	15 mL
I tsp	vanilla	5 mL
⅓ cup	all-purpose flour	75 mL
3 tbsp	unsweetened Dutch-process cocoa powder	45 mL
¾ cup	pecan halves	175 mL

1. In a covered bowl, soak cherries in brandy. Cover and refrigerate for at least 1 week or up to 2 weeks.

2. Preheat oven to 350°F (180°C). In work bowl fitted with metal blade, process brown sugar, butter, granulated sugar and salt until smooth, about 10 seconds. Add egg, honey and vanilla and process until blended, about 20 seconds. Add flour and cocoa powder and process just until incorporated, about 10 seconds. Transfer to a bowl.

3. Drain cherries, reserving brandy. Fold into batter along with pecans. Transfer to prepared loaf pan, smoothing top. Bake in preheated oven until a toothpick inserted in center comes out clean, 20 to 25 minutes. Brush hot cake with reserved brandy. Let cool completely in pan on a wire rack before serving.

Banana Pineapple Cake

Serves 12

This is the moistest cake on earth. I once left it out uncovered and two days later it still was moist!

Tip

If you would like the texture of chunks of pecans, toss a handful in the batter prior to baking.

Variation

Replace the pineapple with ½ cup (125 mL) finely chopped ripe papaya.

- *Preheat oven to 325°F (160°C)*
- *Two 9-inch (23 cm) round cake pans, sprayed with nonstick spray*

3	large very ripe bananas	3
1	can (8 oz/227 mL) crushed pineapple, drained	1
½ cup	pecan halves	125 mL
1¼ cups	vegetable oil	300 mL
3	eggs	3
1½ tsp	vanilla	7 mL
3 cups	all-purpose flour	750 mL
1 tsp	ground cinnamon	5 mL
1 tsp	baking soda	5 mL
1 tsp	salt	5 mL
½ tsp	freshly ground nutmeg	2 mL
	Cream Cheese Icing (optional) (see recipe, page 170)	

1. In work bowl fitted with metal blade, process bananas, pineapple, pecans, oil, eggs and vanilla until smooth, about 10 seconds. Add flour, cinnamon, baking soda, salt and nutmeg. Process just until incorporated, about 10 seconds. Divide batter evenly between prepared pans, spreading to sides.

2. Bake in preheated oven until a toothpick inserted in center comes out clean, 25 to 32 minutes. Let cool in pans on wire racks for 10 minutes. Invert onto racks and remove pans. Let cool completely. Ice with Cream Cheese Icing, if desired.

24 Carrot Cake

I used to work in a restaurant where we called this cake 24 Karrot Kake. Too cutesy I think! But no matter what it's called, this carrot cake is incredibly moist and full of flavor.

Tip

I like to sprinkle grated carrots on the top of the iced cake.

Variation

For 24 cupcakes, divide batter among two greased 12-cup muffin tins. Preheat oven to 350°F (180°C) and reduce baking time to 18 to 22 minutes.

- *Preheat oven to 400°F (200°C)*
- *Two 9-inch (23 cm) round cake pans, sprayed with nonstick spray*

3	carrots, cut into 3-inch (7.5 cm) lengths	3
I cup	pecan halves	250 mL
1¾ cups	granulated sugar	425 mL
¾ cup	vegetable oil	175 mL
3	eggs	3
1¾ cups	all-purpose flour	425 mL
1½ tsp	baking soda	7 mL
¾ tsp	ground cinnamon	4 mL
½ tsp	salt	2 mL
¾ tsp	vanilla	4 mL
I	can (8 oz/227 mL) crushed pineapple, drained	I
I cup	flaked sweetened coconut	250 mL
	Cream Cheese Icing (see recipe, page 170)	

1. In work bowl fitted with shredding blade, shred carrots. Transfer to a bowl.

2. Replace shredding blade with metal blade. Pulse pecans until coarsely chopped, about 10 times. Transfer to bowl with carrots.

3. In same work bowl fitted with metal blade, process sugar, oil and eggs until smooth, about 10 seconds. Add flour, baking soda, cinnamon, salt and vanilla. Process just until incorporated, about 10 seconds. Add pineapple, coconut, pecans and carrots. Process just until incorporated, about 5 seconds. Divide batter evenly between prepared pans, spreading to sides.

4. Bake in preheated oven until a toothpick inserted in center comes out clean, about 22 to 32 minutes. Let cool in pans for 10 minutes. Invert onto racks and remove pans. Let cool completely before icing.

5. Place one cake on a serving plate. Spread with about ½ cup (125 mL) Cream Cheese Icing. Top with second layer. Spread top and sides with remaining icing. Cover loosely with plastic wrap and refrigerate for at least 1 hour or for up to 2 days.

White Cake

| Serves 12 |

This simple, yet tasty cake is perfect for any occasion.

Tip

If the milk is room temperature it incorporates more easily.

Variation

You can substitute 2 whole eggs and 3 egg whites for the 6 egg whites to make a yellow cake.

- *Preheat oven to 350°F (180°C)*
- *13-by 9-inch (3 L) metal baking pan, sprayed with nonstick spray*

1 ¼ cups	unsalted butter, softened	300 mL
2 cups	granulated sugar	500 mL
6	egg whites	6
2 tsp	vanilla	10 mL
3 ½ cups	cake flour	875 mL
1 tbsp	baking powder	15 mL
½ tsp	salt	2 mL
1 cup	whole milk, at room temperature, divided (see Tip, left)	250 mL

1. In work bowl fitted with metal blade, process butter and sugar until creamy, about 20 seconds. With the motor running, pour egg whites through the feed tube in a steady stream until incorporated, about 30 seconds. Add vanilla through the feed tube.

2. In a bowl, blend together cake flour, baking powder and salt. Remove the lid and add half of the flour mixture to work bowl. Replace the lid and process for 20 seconds.

3. With the motor running, add half of the milk through the feed tube and process until smooth, about 20 seconds. Remove the lid and add remaining flour mixture. Replace the lid and process until thick and smooth, about 20 seconds. With the motor running, add remaining milk through the feed tube in a steady stream until incorporated, about 20 seconds. Scrape down bowl. Process just to incorporate, 5 seconds more. Pour into prepared pan, spreading to edges and smoothing top. Bake in preheated oven until golden brown and a toothpick inserted into the center comes out clean, 32 to 38 minutes. Let cool completely in pan on a rack. Frost with either Bittersweet Fudge Frosting (see recipe, page 172) or Buttercream Frosting (see recipe, page 171).

Honey Apple Spice Muffins (page 163)

Cinnamon Pecan Cupcakes

Makes 12 cupcakes

These are perfect cupcakes to serve for brunch or afternoon coffee.

Tips

If butter and cream cheese are not softened prior to use, place in small chunks in the work bowl and process until smooth. Then add sugar.

Double the recipe if desired for 24 cupcakes. Rotate tins during baking to prevent burning on the edges.

Variation

You can also bake this recipe in a parchment-lined 9-by 5-inch (2 L) metal loaf pan. Increase baking time to 40 to 45 minutes.

- *Preheat oven to 375°F (190°C)*
- *One 12-cup muffin tin, lined with paper liners or sprayed with nonstick spray*

½ cup	pecan halves	125 mL
1½ cups	granulated sugar	375 mL
¾ cup	unsalted butter, softened	175 mL
4 oz	cream cheese, softened	125 g
3	eggs	3
1½ tsp	freshly squeezed lemon juice	7 mL
1 tsp	vanilla	5 mL
1⅓ cups	cake flour	325 mL
1½ tsp	ground cinnamon	7 mL
Pinch	salt	Pinch

1. In work bowl fitted with metal blade, process pecans until finely chopped. Transfer to a bowl.

2. In same work bowl fitted with metal blade, process sugar, butter and cream cheese until smooth, about 30 seconds. With the motor running, add eggs, lemon juice and vanilla through the feed tube and process until blended. Remove lid and add cake flour, cinnamon and salt. Cover and process just until incorporated, about 15 seconds. Add pecans and process for 5 seconds.

3. Divide batter evenly into prepared muffin tin. Bake in preheated oven until a toothpick inserted in center comes out clean, 22 to 26 minutes. Let cool in tin for 10 minutes on a wire rack. Transfer to rack to cool completely.

Homemade Ketchup (page 176)

Blueberry Pecan Muffins

Makes 12 muffins

Blueberry muffins are the most popular. Here you have a moist and flavorful muffin that combines the beloved blueberry with pecans for brunch or breakfast in no time.

Tips

If the berries are thawed before adding to the batter, they can turn it an unpleasant blue color.

You can use butter in place of the shortening but your muffins will not be as flaky.

Freeze cooled muffins in a resealable plastic bag for up to 30 days.

Variation

You can substitute the pecans with another nut, if desired.

- *Preheat oven to 375°F (190°C)*
- *One 12-cup muffin tin, sprayed with nonstick spray*

¹⁄₂ cup	pecan halves	125 mL
1 cup	granulated sugar	250 mL
¹⁄₂ cup	cold shortening or unsalted butter, cut into chunks (see Tips, left)	125 mL
2	eggs	2
³⁄₄ cup	milk	175 mL
1 tsp	vanilla	5 mL
2¹⁄₂ cups	cake flour	625 mL
1 tbsp	baking powder	15 mL
¹⁄₂ tsp	salt	2 mL
1 cup	frozen blueberries	250 mL

1. In work bowl fitted with metal blade, pulse pecans until coarsely chopped, about 5 seconds. Transfer to a small bowl. Set aside.

2. In same work bowl fitted with metal blade, process sugar and shortening until smooth, about 30 seconds. With the motor running, add eggs, milk and vanilla through the feed tube. Remove lid and add cake flour, baking powder and salt. Cover and pulse just until incorporated, about 10 times. Transfer to a large bowl. Fold in pecans and blueberries.

3. Divide batter evenly into prepared muffin tin. Bake in preheated oven until a toothpick inserted in center comes out clean, 18 to 22 minutes. Let cool in tin on a wire rack for 15 minutes. Transfer to rack to cool completely.

Honey Apple Spice Muffins

Serve these tasty muffins for breakfast or afternoon tea.

Tips

I like to dust the tops of the muffins with a little sugar and cinnamon prior to baking.

Freeze cooled muffins in a resealable plastic bag for up to 30 days.

Variation

Add ½ cup (125 mL) chopped walnuts to the batter with apple.

- *Preheat oven to 375°F (190°C)*
- *One 12-cup muffin tin, sprayed with nonstick spray*

½	baking apple, cored, peeled and halved	½
1 cup	granulated sugar	250 mL
½ cup	cold shortening or unsalted butter, cut into chunks (see Tips, page 162)	125 mL
2	eggs	2
¾ cup	milk	175 mL
3 tbsp	liquid honey	45 mL
1 tsp	vanilla	5 mL
2½ cups	cake flour	625 mL
1 tbsp	baking powder	15 mL
½ tsp	salt	2 mL
½ tsp	ground cinnamon	2 mL
¼ tsp	freshly ground nutmeg	1 mL

1. In work bowl fitted with metal blade, process apple until coarsely chopped, about 20 seconds. Transfer to a bowl. Set aside.

2. In same work bowl fitted with metal blade, process sugar and shortening until smooth, about 30 seconds. With the motor running, add eggs, milk, honey and vanilla through the feed tube. Remove lid and add cake flour, baking powder, salt, cinnamon and nutmeg. Cover and pulse just until incorporated, about 10 times. Add apple chunks and pulse until mixed, about 5 times.

3. Divide batter evenly into prepared muffin tin. Bake in preheated oven until a toothpick inserted in center comes out clean, 18 to 22 minutes. Let cool in tin on a wire rack for 15 minutes. Transfer to rack to cool completely.

Chocolate Chunk Muffins

Makes 12 muffins

This rich chocolate muffin is very intense. Serve with afternoon tea or coffee.

Tips

Make sure you check the potency of your baking powder. Test it by placing some powder in a glass of water, it should bubble for a few seconds.

Freeze cooled muffins in a resealable plastic bag for up to 30 days.

Variation

Use white chocolate chunks to create a black and white muffin.

- *Preheat oven to 375°F (190°C)*
- *One 12-cup muffin tin, sprayed with nonstick spray*

1 cup	granulated sugar	250 mL
½ cup	cold unsalted butter, cut into chunks	125 mL
2	eggs	2
¾ cup	milk	175 mL
1 tsp	vanilla	5 mL
1½ cups	cake flour	375 mL
¾ cup	all-purpose flour	175 mL
2 tbsp	unsweetened Dutch-process cocoa powder	25 mL
1 tbsp	baking powder	15 mL
½ tsp	ground cinnamon	2 mL
½ tsp	salt	2 mL
3 oz	semisweet chocolate, cut into chunks (about ½ cup/125 mL)	90 g

1. In work bowl fitted with metal blade, process sugar and butter until smooth, about 30 seconds. With the motor running, add eggs, milk and vanilla through the feed tube. Remove lid and add cake and all-purpose flours, cocoa powder, baking powder, cinnamon and salt. Cover and pulse just until incorporated, about 10 times. Add chocolate chunks and pulse until mixed, about 5 times.

2. Divide batter evenly into prepared muffin tin. Bake in preheated oven until a toothpick inserted in center comes out clean, 18 to 22 minutes. Let cool in tin on a wire rack for 15 minutes. Transfer to rack to cool completely.

Pumpkin Muffins

Makes 12 muffins

Fall is not the same without the aroma of hot pumpkin muffins in the air.

Tips

Make sure you drain the pumpkin of any excess liquid.

Freeze cooled muffins in a resealable plastic bag for up to 30 days.

Variation

Add ½ cup (125 mL) chopped pecans after incorporating flour for a nutty taste.

● *Preheat oven to 375°F (190°C)*
● *One 12-cup muffin tin, sprayed with nonstick spray*

I cup	granulated sugar	250 mL
½ cup	cold unsalted butter, cut into chunks	125 mL
¾ cup	Pumpkin Purée (see recipe, page 86) or canned pumpkin purée (not pie filling)	175 mL
2	eggs	2
¾ cup	milk	175 mL
I tsp	vanilla	5 mL
I½ cups	cake flour	375 mL
I cup	all-purpose flour	250 mL
I tbsp	baking powder	15 mL
½ tsp	salt	2 mL
½ tsp	ground cinnamon	2 mL
¼ tsp	freshly ground nutmeg	I mL

1. In work bowl fitted with metal blade, process sugar and butter until smooth, about 20 seconds. With the motor running, add pumpkin, eggs, milk and vanilla through feed tube. Remove lid and add cake and all-purpose flours, baking powder, salt, cinnamon and nutmeg. Cover and pulse just until incorporated, about 10 times.

2. Divide batter evenly into prepared muffin tin. Bake in preheated oven until a toothpick inserted in center comes out clean, 18 to 22 minutes. Let cool in tin on a wire rack for 15 minutes. Transfer to rack to cool completely.

Fresh Savory Herb Scones

Makes 18 scones

I once had a flavorful scone outside of London and kept thinking how delicious it was. I've recreated it here for you to savor.

Tip

Once scones are baked, keep the wedges in the circle after cutting so you have a nice display for your guests.

Variation

You can use an array of fresh herbs such as chives, rosemary or thyme in place of the dill and tarragon.

* *Preheat oven to 450°F (230°C)*
* *Baking sheet, lined with parchment paper*

6 tbsp	shortening or butter (see Tips, page 162)	90 mL
2¼ cups	cake flour	550 mL
1 cup	all-purpose flour	250 mL
¼ cup	granulated sugar	50 mL
4 tsp	baking powder	20 mL
1 tsp	salt	5 mL
1 tsp	grated lemon zest	5 mL
1 tsp	loosely packed fresh dill	5 mL
1 tsp	loosely packed fresh tarragon leaves	5 mL
2	eggs	2
¾ cup	milk	175 mL
1 tsp	freshly squeezed lemon juice	5 mL

1. In work bowl fitted with metal blade, process shortening, cake and all-purpose flours, sugar, baking powder, salt, lemon zest, dill and tarragon until mixture resembles fine crumbs, about 15 seconds. With the motor running, add eggs, milk and lemon juice through the feed tube just until the mixture starts to gather.

2. Scrape dough onto prepared baking sheet and spread out to a 10-inch (25 cm) circle. With a pizza cutter or sharp knife, cut into 18 wedges. Do not separate wedges. Bake in preheated oven until golden brown, 12 to 18 minutes. Serve warm.

Peach Scones

Use fresh ripe peaches for these scones for the most flavor.

Tip
If the mixture seems a bit wet from the peaches you can add up to an additional ½ cup (125 mL) cake flour.

Variation

You may add up to ½ cup (125 mL) chopped pecans or walnuts to the scones with liquid ingredients.

- *Preheat oven to 450°F (230°C)*
- *Baking sheet, lined with parchment paper*

1	peach, pitted and quartered	1
6 tbsp	cold unsalted butter, cut into chunks	90 mL
3¼ cups	cake flour	800 mL
¼ cup	lightly packed brown sugar	50 mL
4 tsp	baking powder	20 mL
1 tsp	ground cinnamon	5 mL
1 tsp	salt	5 mL
2	eggs	2
¾ cup	milk	175 mL

1. In work bowl fitted with metal blade, pulse peach quarters until coarsely chopped. Transfer to a bowl.

2. In same work bowl fitted with metal blade, process butter, cake flour, brown sugar, baking powder, cinnamon and salt until mixture resembles fine crumbs, about 15 seconds. With the motor running, add eggs, milk and peaches through the feed tube just until mixture starts to gather.

3. Scrape dough onto prepared baking sheet and spread out to a 10-inch (25 cm) circle. With a pizza cutter or sharp knife, cut into 18 wedges. Do not separate wedges. Bake in preheated oven until golden brown, 12 to 18 minutes. Serve warm.

Almond Poppy Seed Scones

Makes 18 scones

I think these look great on a spring buffet table.

Tip
Toasting the almonds prior to processing provides a stronger taste.

Variation

You can scoop the dough by spoonfuls into 12 greased muffin tins for larger portions. Bake in a preheated 425°F (220°C) oven for 16 to 20 minutes.

● *Preheat oven to 450°F (230°C)*
● *Baking sheet, lined with parchment paper*

½ cup	slivered almonds, toasted	125 mL
6 tbsp	cold unsalted butter, cut into chunks	90 mL
2¾ cups	all-purpose flour	675 mL
¼ cup	lightly packed brown sugar	50 mL
4 tsp	baking powder	20 mL
1 tsp	poppy seeds	5 mL
1 tsp	salt	5 mL
2	eggs	2
¾ cup	milk	175 mL

1. In work bowl fitted with metal blade, process almonds until finely ground. Transfer to a bowl. Set aside.

2. In same work bowl fitted with metal blade, process butter, flour, brown sugar, baking powder, poppy seeds and salt until mixture resembles fine crumbs, about 15 seconds. Remove lid and add almonds and pulse until incorporated, about 5 times. With the motor running, add eggs and milk through the feed tube just until mixture starts to gather.

2. Scrape dough onto prepared baking sheet and spread out to a 10-inch (25 cm) circle. With a pizza cutter or sharp knife, cut into 18 wedges. Do not separate wedges. Bake in preheated oven until golden brown, 12 to 18 minutes. Serve warm.

Chocolate Chip Scones

Serve these scones to your family either as a dessert or a breakfast item.

Tip
To check for doneness, just lightly touch scones on top; they should be slightly firm.

Variation
Replace ⅓ cup (75 mL) flour with unsweetened cocoa powder for a double chocolate scone.

- *Preheat oven to 450°F (230°C)*
- *Baking sheet, lined with parchment paper*

6 tbsp	cold unsalted butter, cut into chunks	90 mL
3 cups	all-purpose flour	750 mL
¼ cup	granulated sugar	50 mL
4 tsp	baking powder	20 mL
I tsp	salt	5 mL
2	eggs	2
¾ cup	whipping (35%) cream	175 mL
I tsp	vanilla	5 mL
I cup	semisweet chocolate chips	250 mL

1. In work bowl fitted with metal blade, process butter, flour, sugar, baking powder and salt until mixture resembles fine crumbs, about 15 seconds. With the motor running, add eggs, cream and vanilla through the feed tube. Add chocolate chips through the feed tube just until mixture starts to gather.

2. Scrape dough onto prepared baking sheet and spread out to a 10-inch (25 cm) circle. With a pizza cutter or sharp knife, cut into 18 wedges. Do not separate wedges. Bake in preheated oven until golden brown, 12 to 18 minutes. Serve warm.

Cream Cheese Icing

I have been known to eat this icing by the spoonful prior to using. Its texture is perfect and spreads nicely.

Tip

If butter or cream cheese is not softened there will be chunks in the icing.

8 oz	cream cheese, softened, cut into cubes	250 g
¼ cup	unsalted butter, softened, cut into cubes	50 mL
1½ tsp	vanilla	7 mL
2½ cups	confectioner's (icing) sugar	625 mL

1. In work bowl fitted with metal blade, process cream cheese and butter until smooth, about 20 seconds. With motor running, add vanilla through the feed tube until incorporated. Scrape down bowl. Add confectioner's sugar and process until smooth, about 30 seconds.

Buttercream Frosting

The food processor makes the creamiest and smoothest frostings! You don't have to sift the confectioner's sugar.

Tips

If you would like to use this as a glaze you can add additional milk to thin the texture.

For a stiffer frosting add additional confectioner's sugar after adding milk.

Variations

Add 1 cup (250 mL) toasted flaked coconut for a flavorful frosting.

Use the same amount of vanilla in place of almond extract for a vanilla buttercream.

½ cup	unsalted butter, softened, cut into cubes	125 mL
3½ cups	confectioner's (icing) sugar	875 mL
¼ cup	milk	50 mL
2 tsp	almond extract	10 mL

1. In work bowl fitted with metal blade, process butter until smooth, about 30 seconds. Scrape down bowl. Add confectioner's sugar and process until it just begins to gather, about 15 seconds. With the motor running, drizzle milk and almond extract through the feed tube and process until smooth, about 30 seconds.

Bittersweet Fudge Frosting

*When it's my birthday,
the only cake I still want
my Mom to make is a
chocolate one with this
frosting!*

4 oz	bittersweet chocolate, chopped	125 g
½ cup	unsalted butter, softened, cut into cubes	125 mL
4 cups	confectioner's (icing) sugar	1 L
1 tsp	rum extract	5 mL

1. In a microwave-safe bowl, microwave chocolate on Medium, stirring every 30 seconds, until soft and almost melted, 1 to 1½ minutes. Stir until completely melted and smooth. Let cool slightly.

2. In work bowl fitted with metal blade, process butter until smooth, about 30 seconds. Scrape down bowl. Add confectioner's sugar and process until it just begins to gather, about 15 seconds. With the motor running, add chocolate and rum extract through the feed tube and process until smooth, about 30 seconds.

Sauces

Smoked Chili Sauce 174

Fresh Herb Tomato Dipping Sauce. 175

Homemade Ketchup 176

Garden Fresh Pesto Sauce. 177

Roasted Red Pepper Velvet Sauce 178

Tomato Sauce 179

Raspberry Sauce 180

Apple Raisin Sauce 181

Smoked Chili Sauce

**Makes about
2 cups (500 mL)**

*This sauce is so versatile.
You can use it as a
barbecue sauce or a
filling in Mini Chicken
Puffs (see recipe,
page 24).*

Tips

Sauce keeps well,
covered and refrigerated,
for up to 3 weeks.

Using two types of
vinegars here prevents
a bitter aftertaste.

Variation

Omit the chipotle
peppers for a basic
chili sauce.

I cup	rice vinegar	250 mL
I cup	cider vinegar	250 mL
2 tsp	ground cloves	10 mL
I tsp	ground allspice	5 mL
I	onion, cut into quarters	I
10	cloves garlic	10
I cup	lightly packed brown sugar	250 mL
1½ cups	Homemade Ketchup (see recipe, page 176) or store-bought	375 mL
I	can (7 oz/215 g) chipotle peppers in adobo sauce, drained	I
2 tbsp	fresh cilantro leaves	25 mL
I tbsp	Worcestershire sauce	15 mL

1. In a deep saucepan over medium heat, combine rice vinegar, cider vinegar, cloves and allspice. Bring to a low boil. Set aside.

2. In work bowl fitted with metal blade, process onion, garlic, brown sugar, ketchup, chipotle peppers, cilantro and Worcestershire sauce until finely chopped, about 30 seconds. Add to cider mixture and bring to a gentle boil over medium heat. Reduce heat and boil gently, stirring often, until reduced to a thick sauce, about 1 hour. Let cool.

Fresh Herb Tomato Dipping Sauce

Spread this sauce over a French baguette instead of butter.

Tips

Cut the tomatoes in half crosswise and squeeze out all the seeds. This is a fast seeding method.

This recipe works best with ¼ cup (50 mL) chopped shallot. One shallot about 1¾ inches (4.5 cm) in diameter will yield about ¼ cup (50 mL) when chopped. If you have a different size shallot, adjust the amount accordingly.

Sauce keeps well, covered and refrigerated, for up to 1 week.

Variation

Use an herb such as dill or tarragon in place of rosemary.

4	Roma tomatoes, cored and seeded (about 12 oz/375 g) (see Tips, left)	4
1	shallot (about ¼ cup/50 mL) (see Tips, left)	1
1 tbsp	fresh rosemary leaves	15 mL
1	clove garlic	1
½ tsp	freshly ground black pepper	2 mL
⅔ cup	dry white wine	150 mL
¼ cup	red wine vinegar	50 mL
¼ cup	olive oil	50 mL
½ tsp	salt	2 mL
	Granulated sugar (optional)	
1	large fresh baguette	1

1. In work bowl fitted with metal blade, pulse tomatoes, shallot, rosemary, garlic and pepper until chunky, about 20 times.

2. Transfer mixture to a small saucepan over medium heat. Cook, stirring, until onion is soft, about 5 minutes. Add wine, vinegar, olive oil and salt. Reduce heat and boil gently, stirring occasionally, until reduced to a thick sauce, 20 to 25 minutes. If the tomatoes are tart, season with up to 1 tbsp (15 mL) sugar.

2. Cut baguette into 1-inch (2.5 cm) slices. Serve warm spread over baguette or use as a dipping sauce.

Homemade Ketchup

*I had never thought
of making my own
ketchup until I read
the ingredients on the
label of a store-bought
bottle. I couldn't even
pronounce half of them,
so I figured that they
must be preservatives
and stabilizers. I believe
that if these ingredients
aren't available at a
supermarket, you
shouldn't be eating
them.*

Tips

Store ketchup in a
covered container in
the refrigerator for
up to 2 months.

When seeding the
tomatoes, just core
them, cut them in half
crosswise and squeeze
them like a sponge.
The seeds extract fast
this way.

Variation

Combine equal parts
Homemade Ketchup
and Traditional
Mayonnaise (see recipe,
page 36) for a simple
salad dressing.

3	vine-ripened tomatoes (each about 6 oz/175 g), cored, cut in half and seeded (see Tips, left)	3
1/2	onion, quartered	1/2
1/2 cup	tomato paste	125 mL
1/2 cup	light corn syrup	125 mL
1/2 cup	vinegar	125 mL
1 tbsp	granulated sugar	15 mL
1 tsp	salt	5 mL
1/4 tsp	onion powder	1 mL
1/8 tsp	garlic powder	0.5 mL

1. In work bowl fitted with metal blade, process tomatoes and onion until smooth, about 2 minutes.

2. Place mixture in a deep saucepan. Add tomato paste, corn syrup, vinegar, sugar, salt, onion powder and garlic powder. Bring to a boil over medium heat. Reduce heat and simmer, stirring occasionally, until thickened, for 20 minutes. Transfer to a bowl or container and let cool, uncovered, to room temperature.

Garden Fresh Pesto Sauce

**Makes 1½ cups
(375 mL)**

If you're lucky enough to have fresh basil growing in your garden, this recipe is the perfect use. Serve over pasta with cut-up pieces of chicken.

Tip

Basil and parsley need to be washed well to remove all sand and dirt. Be sure to dry them well. If the basil and parsley are not dried completely, the pesto will have a watered-down taste. I like to use an herb spinner to get out the excess water.

Variation

For a nutty taste, add ½ cup (125 mL) toasted pine nuts when you pulse the pesto for the last time.

6 oz	Parmesan cheese, cut into chunks	175 g
2 cups	tightly packed fresh basil leaves (see Tip, left)	500 mL
¾ cup	extra virgin olive oil, divided	175 mL
8	sprigs Italian parsley (see Tip, left)	8
4	cloves garlic	4
Pinch	salt	Pinch
Pinch	freshly ground black pepper	Pinch

1. In work bowl fitted with metal blade, with the motor running, add Parmesan cheese through the feed tube and process until grated. Transfer to a bowl. Set aside.

2. In same work bowl fitted with metal blade, process basil leaves, ½ cup (125 mL) of the olive oil, parsley and garlic until finely chopped, about 30 seconds. Season with salt and pepper.

3. Add remaining olive oil and the Parmesan cheese and pulse until well blended, 2 to 3 seconds.

4. If not using immediately, scrape pesto into a jar or plastic container. Top with ¼ cup (50 mL) olive oil and refrigerate for up to 1 week or freeze for up to 1 year. Place in the refrigerator for 1 day to defrost.

Roasted Red Pepper Velvet Sauce

Serve this luxurious sauce with any seafood or toss it with cooked seafood for a tasty sandwich filling or salad. It's easy to roast your own red peppers to achieve the characteristic smoky flavor. But if time is limited, jarred roasted peppers are available in most supermarkets.

Tips

If red bell peppers are on sale, purchase a few pounds and roast them all on the grill or preheated broiler, turning two or three times, until charred. Place in a plastic bag to steam for 20 minutes. Then peel the blackened skins off and remove the stems and seeds.

Store peppers in jars filled with olive oil for up to 6 months.

Sauce keeps, covered and refrigerated, for up to 1 week.

Variation

Try soy sauce in place of the Worcestershire sauce.

2	large red bell peppers, roasted, or 1 jar (7 oz/210 g) whole roasted red peppers	2
¾ cup	Traditional Mayonnaise (see recipe, page 36) or store-bought	175 mL
2 tbsp	freshly squeezed lemon juice	25 mL
1 tbsp	grated fresh gingerroot	15 mL
2 tsp	Worcestershire sauce	10 mL
½ tsp	freshly ground black pepper	2 mL
¼ tsp	salt	1 mL
6	drops hot pepper sauce	6

1. In work bowl fitted with metal blade, add peppers and pulse until finely chopped, about 10 times. Add mayonnaise, lemon juice, ginger, Worcestershire sauce, pepper and salt. Process until blended, about 10 seconds. Transfer mixture to a bowl. Stir in hot pepper sauce. Taste and adjust seasonings. Cover with plastic wrap or transfer to an airtight container until ready to use.

Tomato Sauce

*In California we tend
to have tomato plants
growing like weeds.
I try to make a batch
or two of this sauce to
use when tomatoes are
pricey. You can make
this when tomatoes
are a bargain or they're
in season in your neck
of the woods.*

Tips
Leftover sauce can be
cooled and frozen in an
airtight container for
up to 2 months.

If tomatoes are not
sweet enough you can
add up to 2 tsp (10 mL)
additional sugar.

Variation

For a meat sauce, add
2 lbs (1 kg) cooked
ground beef, drained
of fat, in Step 4.

2	large onions, cut into quarters	2
I	carrot, cut into 1-inch (2.5 cm) pieces	I
I	stalk celery, peeled and cut into 1-inch (2.5 cm) pieces	I
3	cloves garlic, cut in half	3
¼ cup	loosely packed basil leaves	50 mL
¼ cup	unsalted butter	50 mL
¼ cup	olive oil	50 mL
4 lbs	Roma tomatoes, peeled, cored and seeded (28 to 36)	2 kg
1½ cups	vegetable stock	375 mL
I tsp	granulated sugar	5 mL
	Salt and freshly ground black pepper	

1. In work bowl fitted with metal blade, process onions, carrot, celery, garlic and basil until coarsely chopped, about 15 times.

2. In a large saucepan over medium heat, melt butter and oil. Add onion mixture. Sauté until vegetables are soft and basil is wilted, 8 to 10 minutes.

3. In same work bowl fitted with metal blade, pulse tomatoes, in batches, until coarsely chopped, about 10 times. Add tomatoes to saucepan.

4. Add stock, sugar and pinch each salt and pepper to saucepan. Reduce heat to low and simmer, stirring, until thickened, about 1 hour. Check seasoning and add more salt and pepper to taste.

Raspberry Sauce

Makes 1½ cups (375 mL)

I use this sauce in the Macadamia-Crusted Salmon (see recipe, page 64). You can also spoon it over ice cream.

Tips

Store sauce, cooled completely, covered and refrigerated, for up to 5 days.

If you would like a seedless sauce, strain prior to heating.

Variation

You can use a bag of mixed berries, about 2 cups (500 mL) in place of the raspberries.

1	bag (10 oz/300 g) frozen raspberries, thawed (about 2 cups/500 mL)	1
1 cup	granulated sugar	250 mL
¼ cup	cornstarch	50 mL
2 tsp	freshly squeezed lemon juice	10 mL

1. In work bowl fitted with metal blade, process raspberries, sugar, cornstarch and lemon juice until smooth, about 1 minute.

2. Transfer mixture to a saucepan over medium heat. Heat mixture, stirring constantly, until it starts to boil and thicken, about 10 minutes. Place in a bowl.

Apple Raisin Sauce

Makes 2 cups (500 mL)

I like to serve this with scones or over ice cream.

Tips

Store sauce, cooled completely, covered and refrigerated for up to 3 days.

If the apples are not baking apples they may break down too much and create applesauce. Cortland or Granny Smith are good choices for baking apples.

Variation

You can use the same amount of dried cranberries in place of the raisins.

3	baking apples, peeled, cored and quartered (see Tips, left)	3
½ cup	granulated sugar	125 mL
1 tsp	ground cinnamon	5 mL
½ tsp	ground nutmeg	2 mL
½ cup	golden raisins	125 mL
2 tbsp	rum (optional)	25 mL

1. In work bowl fitted with slicing blade, slice apples.

2. In a saucepan over medium heat, combine apples, sugar, cinnamon and nutmeg. Cook, stirring, until the mixture starts to break down and bubbles slightly, about 5 minutes. Remove from heat and stir in raisins and rum, if using. Serve warm or cold.

Library and Archives Canada Cataloguing in Publication

Geary, George
    125 best food processor recipes / George Geary.

ISBN 0-7788-0123-3

1. Food processor cookery. I. Title. II. Title: One hundred twenty-five best
food processor recipes.

TX840.F6G42 2005   641.5'892   C2005-902583-2

Index

v = variation

A

All-Butter Pie Pastry, 134
All-Rich Butter Cookies, 118
Almond paste
  Pear Almond Cream Tarts, 141
Almonds, toasting, 27
  Almond Poppy Seed Scones,
    168
  Savory Chicken Cheese Balls,
    27
  Strawberry Almond Cookies,
    122
  The Perfect Fudgey Brownie,
    131
  Vegetable Almond Medley,
    94
Appetizers
  Black Bean Chipotle Dip, 28
  Crispy Chicken Cakes with
    Fresh Dill Mayonnaise, 25
  Crab Feta Mushrooms, 18
  Deviled Eggs with Caviar, 23
  Grande Beef Nachos, 22
  Herbed Seafood Cakes (v), 25
  Hummus for a Crowd, 29
  Mini Chicken Puffs, 24
  Mini Meatballs with Garlic
    Tomato Sauce, 20
  Mini Vegetarian Puffs (v), 24
  New Orleans Bourbon
    Chicken (v), 69
  Peach Mango Salsa, 33
  Roasted Corn and Pepper
    Salsa, 32
  Roasted Red Pepper
    Guacamole Dip, 30
  Salmon Herb Mousse on
    Stone-Ground Crackers, 16
  Savory Chicken Cheese Balls,
    27
  Shrimp Pâté with Leeks, 17
  Thai Beef Skewers in Peanut
    Sauce, 19
  Tomatillo Onion Avocado
    Salsa, 31
  Traditional Salsa, 34

Apples
  Apple Crisp with Crumb
    Topping, 148
  Apple Pockets, 144
  Apple Raisin Sauce, 181
  Apple Spice Pie, 136
  Cinnamon Apple Shortbread,
    128
  Honey Apple Spice Muffins,
    163
  Pear Pandowdy (v), 146
Apricots
  Savory Chicken Cheese Balls
    (v), 27
Asparagus
  Hearty Cauliflower and
    Asparagus Soup, 60
Avocados
  Avocado Tamarind Cashew
    Dressing, 49
  Cold Shrimp Salad, 65
  Roasted Red Pepper
    Guacamole Dip, 30
  Tomatillo Onion Avocado
    Salsa, 31

B

Bacon
  Deviled Eggs with Caviar, 23
  Navy Bean Soup, 58
Baked Beef Burgundy, 81
Banana Pineapple Cake, 157
Basil
  Chicken Rockefeller (v), 76
  Garden Fresh Pesto Sauce,
    177
  Grilled Portobello Mushrooms
    with Balsamic Vinegar, 87
  Hearty Cauliflower and
    Asparagus Soup, 60
  Pepper Pasta Salad, 44
  Roasted Tomato Parmesan
    Soup, 56
  Sun-Dried Tomato Pesto
    Bread, 106
  Tomato Basil Tart, 93
  Tomato Sauce, 179
Beef
  Baked Beef Burgundy, 81

Thai Beef Skewers in Peanut
    Sauce, 19
Beef, ground
  Fast and Easy Meat Loaf, 77
  Grande Beef Nachos, 22
  Mini Meatballs with Garlic
    Tomato Sauce, 20
  Tomato Sauce (v), 179
  Turkey Meatballs (v), 74
Bell peppers, *see* Peppers, bell
Berry Pie, 137
Bittersweet Fudge Frosting, 172
Black beans
  Black Bean Chipotle Dip, 28
  Grande Beef Nachos, 22
Blackberries
  Berry Pie, 137
Blueberries
  Blueberry Pecan Muffins, 162
  Raspberry Vinaigrette (v), 50
Blue cheese, about, 12
  Blue Cheese Peanut Coleslaw,
    41
  Blue Cheese Peppercorn
    Dressing, 48
  Crab Feta Mushrooms (v), 18
  Potato Cheese Soufflé (v), 90
  Stuffed Chicken Breasts (v), 75
Bourbon
  New Orleans Bourbon
    Chicken, 69
Brandy
  Caramelized Onion and
    Mushroom Soup, 52
Breads, *see also* Rolls
  California Wine and Cheese
    Bread, 100
  Fresh Bread Crumbs, 26
  Fresh Tarragon Dill Bread, 104
  Honey Whole Wheat
    Sunflower Bread, 102
  Roasted Chicken Garlic Salad
    Sandwiches, 42
  Sun-Dried Tomato Pesto
    Bread, 106
Broccoli
  Hearty Cauliflower and
    Asparagus Soup (v), 60

Vegetable Almond Medley, 94
Brownies, see also Cookies
    Chocolate Raspberry
        Brownies, 132
    The Perfect Fudgey Brownie,
        131
Butter, about, 12
    Honey Butter, 40
    Tarragon Dill Butter, 39
Buttercream Frosting, 171
Buttermilk
    Blue Cheese Peppercorn
        Dressing, 48
Buttery Tart Pastry, 139

C

Cabbage
    Blue Cheese Peanut Coleslaw,
        41
Cakes
    Banana Pineapple Cake, 157
    24 Carrot Cake, 158
    White Cake, 160
California Wine and Cheese
    Bread, 100
Capers
    Salmon Herb Mousse on
        Stone-Ground Crackers, 16
    Tuscan Pork Chops, 80
Caramel Chocolate Tarts, 142
Caramelized Onion and
    Mushroom Soup, 52
Carrots
    Baked Beef Burgundy, 81
    Blue Cheese Peanut Coleslaw,
        41
    Navy Bean Soup, 58
    Roasted Vegetables, 97
    Tomato Sauce, 179
    24 Carrot Cake, 158
    Vegetable Almond Medley, 94
Cashews
    Avocado Tamarind Cashew
        Dressing, 49
    Three-Nut Cheesecake, 152
Cauliflower
    Hearty Cauliflower and
        Asparagus Soup, 60
Caviar
    Deviled Eggs with Caviar, 23
Chanterelle Oyster Bisque Soup,
    55

Cheddar, about, 11
    Cheddar Cheese Rolls, 110
    Grande Beef Nachos, 22
    Mini Chicken Puffs, 24
    Potatoes au Gratin, 92
Cheese, about, 11, see also
    individual varieties
    Cheddar Cheese Rolls, 110
    Eggplant Parmesan, 96
    Grande Beef Nachos, 22
    Portobello Mushroom
        Lasagna, 88
    Potatoes au Gratin, 92
    Tomato Basil Tart, 93
Cheesecakes
    Citrus Bliss Cheesecake, 151
    Deep Dark Chocolate Fudge
        Cheesecake, 154
    Lemon Mist Cheesecake,
        150
    Three-Nut Cheesecake, 152
Cherries
    Chocolate Cherry Loaf, 156
Chicken
    Hot and Spicy BBQ Rub, 83
    Jerk Chicken, 70
    Thai Beef Skewers in Peanut
        Sauce (v), 19
Chicken, breasts
    Chicken Rockefeller, 76
    Drunken Fresh Herb
        Marinade, 84
    Mushroom-Crusted Chicken,
        72
    New Orleans Bourbon
        Chicken, 69
    Potato Chip Chicken, 73
    Stuffed Chicken Breasts, 75
Chicken, cooked
    Crispy Chicken Cakes with
        Fresh Dill Mayonnaise, 25
    Mini Chicken Puffs, 24
    Roasted Chicken Garlic Salad
        Sandwiches, 42
    Savory Chicken Cheese Balls,
        27
Chicken, wings
    New Orleans Bourbon
        Chicken (v), 69
Chickpeas
    Hummus for a Crowd, 29

Chile peppers
    Chipotle Mayonnaise, 38
    Drunken Fresh Herb
        Marinade, 84
    Jerk Chicken, 70
    Red Hot Chili, 78
    Roasted Corn and Pepper
        Salsa, 32
    Tomatillo Onion Avocado
        Salsa, 31
    Traditional Salsa, 34
Chipotle Mayonnaise
    Thousand Island Dressing (v),
        47
Chipotle peppers
    Chipotle Mayonnaise, 38
    Smoked Chili Sauce, 174
Chocolate, about, 13
    Bittersweet Fudge Frosting, 172
    Caramel Chocolate Tarts, 142
    Chocolate Cherry Loaf, 156
    Chocolate Chunk Muffins, 164
    Chocolate Raspberry
        Brownies, 132
    Chocolate Tart Pastry, 140
    Deep Dark Chocolate Fudge
        Cheesecake, 154
    The Perfect Fudgey Brownie,
        131
Chocolate chips
    Chocolate Chip Scones, 169
    Pecan Pumpkin Harvest
        Cookies, 123
    Quadruple Chocolate Chunk
        Cookies, 130
Cinnamon Apple Shortbread,
    128
Cinnamon Pecan Cupcakes, 161
Citrus Bliss Cheesecake, 151
Clams
    New England Clam Chowder,
        54
Cocoa
    Chocolate Cherry Loaf, 156
    Chocolate Chip Scones (v), 169
    Chocolate Chunk Muffins, 164
    Chocolate Raspberry
        Brownies, 132
    Chocolate Tart Pastry, 140
    Quadruple Chocolate Chunk
        Cookies, 130

Coconut
  Buttercream Frosting (v), 171
  24 Carrot Cake, 158
Coffee granules
  Caramel Chocolate Tarts, 142
Cold Shrimp Salad, 65
Coleslaw
  Blue Cheese Peanut Coleslaw, 41
Cooked chicken, *see* Chicken, cooked
Cookies, *see also* Brownies
  All-Rich Butter Cookies, 118
  Cinnamon Apple Shortbread, 128
  Lemon Citrus Cookies, 120
  Oatmeal Cinnamon Raisin Cookies, 124
  Orange Zest Cookies, 121
  Peanut Sandwich Cookies, 126
  Pecan Pumpkin Harvest Cookies, 123
  Quadruple Chocolate Chunk Cookies, 130
  Strawberry Almond Cookies, 122
  Sugar and Spice Cookies, 129
Corn
  Roasted Corn and Pepper Salsa, 32
Crab
  Crab Feta Mushrooms, 18
  Herbed Seafood Cakes (v), 25
Cranberries, dried
  Apple Raisin Sauce (v), 181
  Oatmeal Cinnamon Raisin Cookies (v), 124
  Strawberry Almond Cookies (v), 122
Cream cheese, about, 11
  Black Bean Chipotle Dip, 28
  Blue Cheese Peppercorn Dressing, 48
  Cinnamon Pecan Cupcakes, 161
  Citrus Bliss Cheesecake, 151
  Cream Cheese Icing, 170
  Deep Dark Chocolate Fudge Cheesecake, 154
  Lemon Mist Cheesecake, 150
  Peanut Sandwich Cookies, 126
  Roasted Chicken Garlic Salad Sandwiches, 42

  Salmon Herb Mousse on Stone-Ground Crackers, 16
  Savory Chicken Cheese Balls, 27
  Shrimp Pâté with Leeks, 17
  Three-Nut Cheesecake, 152
Cream Cheese Icing, 170
  Banana Pineapple Cake, 157
  24 Carrot Cake, 158
Creamy French Salad Dressing, 46
Crispy Chicken Cakes with Fresh Dill Mayonnaise, 25
Crusty French Rolls, 114
Cupcakes
  Cinnamon Pecan Cupcakes, 161
  24 Carrot Cake (v), 158

D
Deep Dark Chocolate Fudge Cheesecake, 154
Deviled Eggs with Caviar, 23
Dill
  Fresh Dill Mayonnaise, 37
  Fresh Tarragon Dill Bread, 104
  Tarragon Dill Butter, 39
Dips, *see also* Appetizers
  Black Bean Chipotle Dip, 28
  Hummus for a Crowd, 29
  Roasted Red Pepper Guacamole Dip, 30
Dough, rolling out, 134
Dressings, *see* Salad dressings
Drunken Fresh Herb Marinade, 84

E
Eggplant Parmesan, 96
Eggs, about, 12
  Chipotle Mayonnaise, 38
  Deviled Eggs with Caviar, 23
  Egg Salad Spread, 43
  Fresh Dill Mayonnaise, 37
  pasteurized, about, 36
  Potato Cheese Soufflé, 90
  Traditional Mayonnaise, 36

F
Fast and Easy Meat Loaf, 77
Fast and Easy Pizza Dough, 116
Feta cheese
  Crab Feta Mushrooms, 18
  Stuffed Chicken Breasts, 75

Fish, *see also* Seafood and individual varieties
  Macadamia-Crusted Salmon, 64
  Seafood Pâté, 66
Flavored butters, *see* Butter
French Onion Soup, 62
Fresh Bread Crumbs, 26
  Chicken Rockefeller, 76
  Crispy Chicken Cakes with Fresh Dill Mayonnaise, 25
  Fast and Easy Meat Loaf, 77
  Mini Meatballs with Garlic Tomato Sauce, 20
  Turkey Meatballs, 74
  Vegetable Almond Medley, 94
Fresh Dill Mayonnaise, 37
  Crispy Chicken Cakes with Fresh Dill Mayonnaise, 25
  Roasted Chicken Garlic Salad Sandwiches, 42
Fresh Herb Tomato Dipping Sauce, 175
Fresh Savory Herb Scones, 166
Fresh Tarragon Dill Bread, 104
Frostings
  Bittersweet Fudge Frosting, 172
  Buttercream Frosting, 171
  Cream Cheese Icing, 170
Fruits, processing, 13
  slicing and shredding, 13

G
Garden Fresh Pesto Sauce, 177
Grande Beef Nachos, 22
Grapes
  Savory Chicken Cheese Balls, 27
Grilled Portobello Mushrooms with Balsamic Vinegar, 87
Ground beef, *see* Beef, ground
Ground turkey, *see* Turkey, ground
Green peppers, *see* Peppers, bell; Chile peppers; Jalapeño peppers

H
Ham
  Egg Salad Spread, 43
  Navy Bean Soup, 58
  Pepper Pasta Salad (v), 44
  Stuffed Chicken Breasts, 75

Hazelnuts
    Caramel Chocolate Tarts (v), 142
    Pecan Pumpkin Harvest Cookies (v), 123
Hearty Cauliflower and Asparagus Soup, 60
Herbed Seafood Cakes (v), 25
Herbs, about, 13
Homemade Ketchup, 176
    Smoked Chili Sauce, 174
Honey Apple Spice Muffins, 163
Honey Butter, 40
Honey Whole Wheat Sunflower Bread, 102
Hot and Spicy BBQ Rub, 83
Hummus for a Crowd, 29

I

Icings, *see* Frostings

J

Jack cheese, about, 11, *see also* Monterey Jack cheese
Jalapeño peppers
    Red Hot Chili, 78
    Roasted Corn and Pepper Salsa (v), 32
    Roasted Red Pepper Guacamole Dip, 30
    Traditional Salsa (v), 34
Jamaican Seafood Rub, 82
Jerk Chicken, 70

K

Ketchup
    Homemade Ketchup, 176
    Smoked Chili Sauce, 174

L

Leeks, cleaning, 53
    Caramelized Onion and Mushroom Soup (v), 52
    New England Clam Chowder, 54
    Potato Leek Cheese Soup, 53
Lemons
    Citrus Bliss Cheesecake, 151
    Lemon Citrus Cookies, 120
    Lemon Mist Cheesecake, 150
Liqueur
    Caramel Chocolate Tarts, 142
    Pumpkin Pecan Pie (v), 138

M

Macadamia-Crusted Salmon, 64
Mango
    Peach Mango Salsa, 33
Marinades
    Drunken Fresh Herb Marinade, 84
Mayonnaise
    Blue Cheese Peanut Coleslaw, 41
    Blue Cheese Peppercorn Dressing, 48
    Chipotle Mayonnaise, 38
    Cold Shrimp Salad, 65
    Crispy Chicken Cakes with Fresh Dill Mayonnaise, 25
    Deviled Eggs with Caviar, 23
    Egg Salad Spread, 43
    Fresh Dill Mayonnaise, 37
    Roasted Chicken Garlic Salad Sandwiches, 42
    Roasted Red Pepper Velvet Sauce, 178
    The Perfect Fudgey Brownie, 131
    Thousand Island Dressing, 47
    Tomato Basil Tart, 93
    Traditional Mayonnaise, 36
Meatballs
    Mini Meatballs with Garlic Tomato Sauce, 20
    Turkey Meatballs, 74
Meat loaf
    Fast and Easy Meat Loaf, 77
Mini Chicken Puffs, 24
Mini Meatballs with Garlic Tomato Sauce, 20
Mini Vegetarian Puffs (v), 24
Monterey Jack cheese, *see also* Jack Cheese
    California Wine and Cheese Bread, 100
    Grande Beef Nachos, 22
    Cheddar Cheese Rolls (v), 110
    French Onion Soup, 62
    Potato Leek Cheese Soup, 53
Mozzarella, about, 11
    Eggplant Parmesan, 96
    Tomato Basil Tart, 93
Muffins, *see also* Quick Breads

Almond Poppy Seed Scones (v), 168
Blueberry Pecan Muffins, 162
Chocolate Chunk Muffins, 164
Honey Apple Spice Muffins, 163
Pumpkin Muffins, 165
Mushrooms
    Baked Beef Burgundy, 81
    Caramelized Onion and Mushroom Soup, 52
    Chanterelle Oyster Bisque Soup, 55
    Crab Feta Mushrooms, 18
    Grilled Portobello Mushrooms with Balsamic Vinegar, 87
    Mini Vegetarian Puffs (v), 24
    Mushroom-Crusted Chicken, 72
    Mushroom-Stuffed Pork Chops, 79
    New England Clam Chowder (v), 54
    Portobello Mushroom Lasagna, 88

N

Nachos
    Grande Beef Nachos, 22
Navy Bean Soup, 58
Neufchâtel cheese, about, 11
New England Clam Chowder, 54
New Orleans Bourbon Chicken, 69
Nuts, about, 12, *see also* individual varieties
    All-Rich Butter Cookies (v), 118
    Apple Crisp with Crumb Topping (v), 148
    Macadamia-Crusted Salmon, 64
    Three-Nut Cheesecake, 152

O

Oatmeal Cinnamon Raisin Cookies, 124
Oil, about, 13
Onions
    Baked Beef Burgundy, 81
    Caramelized Onion and Mushroom Soup, 52
    French Onion Soup, 62
    New England Clam Chowder, 54

Potato Leek Cheese Soup (v), 53
Oranges
    Citrus Bliss Cheesecake, 151
    Orange Zest Cookies, 121
Oysters
    Chanterelle Oyster Bisque Soup, 55

P

Papaya
    Banana Pineapple Cake (v), 157
Parmesan, about, 11
    Creamy French Salad Dressing, 46
    Eggplant Parmesan, 96
    Garden Fresh Pesto Sauce, 177
    Grilled Portobello Mushrooms with Balsamic Vinegar (v), 87
    Pepper Pasta Salad, 44
    Portobello Mushroom Lasagna, 88
    Roasted Tomato Parmesan Soup, 56
    Tuscan Pork Chops, 80
Pasta
    Pepper Pasta Salad, 44
    Portobello Mushroom Lasagna, 88
Pastry
    All-Butter Pie Pastry, 134
    Buttery Tart Pastry, 139
    Chocolate Tart Pastry, 140
    Dough, rolling out, 134
    Savory Buttery Tart Pastry (v), 139
    Spiced Pastry, 135
Pâtés
    Seafood Pâté, 66
    Shrimp Pâté with Leeks, 17
Peaches
    Peach Mango Salsa, 33
    Peach Scones, 167
    Pear Almond Cream Tarts (v), 141
Peanut Sandwich Cookies, 126
Pears
    Apple Pockets (v), 144
    Cinnamon Apple Shortbread (v), 128
    Pear Almond Cream Tarts, 141
    Pear Pandowdy, 146

Pecans
    Banana Pineapple Cake, 157
    Blueberry Pecan Muffins, 162
    Chocolate Cherry Loaf, 156
    Cinnamon Pecan Cupcakes, 161
    Peach Scones (v), 167
    Pecan Pumpkin Harvest Cookies, 123
    Pecan Yams, 98
    Pumpkin Muffins (v), 165
    Pumpkin Pecan Pie, 138
    Roasted Pecan Pumpkin Soup, 59
    Three-Nut Cheesecake, 152
    24 Carrot Cake, 158
Pepper Pasta Salad, 44
Peppers, bell
    Black Bean Chipotle Dip, 28
    Blue Cheese Peanut Coleslaw, 41
    Fast and Easy Meat Loaf, 77
    Pepper Pasta Salad, 44
    Red Hot Chili, 78
    Roasted Red Pepper Guacamole Dip, 30
    Roasted Red Pepper Velvet Sauce, 178
    Roasted Vegetables, 97
Pies and tarts
    All-Butter Pie Pastry, 134
    Apple Spice Pie, 136
    Berry Pie, 137
    Buttery Tart Pastry, 139
    Caramel Chocolate Tarts, 142
    Chocolate Tart Pastry, 140
    Dough, rolling out, 134
    Pear Almond Cream Tarts, 141
    Pumpkin Pecan Pie, 138
    Savory Buttery Tart Pastry (v), 139
    Spiced Pastry, 135
    Tomato Basil Tart, 93
Pineapples
    Banana Pineapple Cake, 157
    Pecan Yams (v), 98
    24 Carrot Cake, 158
Pine nuts
    Garden Fresh Pesto Sauce (v), 177
    Roasted Pecan Pumpkin Soup (v), 59

Stuffed Chicken Breasts, 75
Pinto beans
    Black Bean Chipotle Dip (v), 28
    Grande Beef Nachos, 22
Pizza
    Fast and Easy Pizza Dough, 116
Pork
    Baked Beef Burgundy (v), 81
    New England Clam Chowder, 54
Pork chops
    Mushroom-Stuffed Pork Chops, 79
    Tuscan Pork Chops, 80
Portobello Mushroom Lasagna, 88
Potato Chip Chicken, 73
Potatoes
    New England Clam Chowder, 54
    Potato Cheese Soufflé, 90
    Potato Leek Cheese Soup, 53
    Potato Rolls, 108
    Potatoes au Gratin, 92
    Roasted Vegetables, 97
Provolone cheese, about, 11
    Chicken Rockefeller, 76
    Mushroom-Stuffed Pork Chops (v), 79
    Portobello Mushroom Lasagna, 88
Puff pastry
    Apple Pockets, 144
    Mini Chicken Puffs, 24
Pumpkin
    Pecan Pumpkin Harvest Cookies, 123
    Pumpkin Muffins, 165
    Pumpkin Pecan Pie, 138
    Roasted Pecan Pumpkin Soup, 59
    Pumpkin Purée, 86

Q

Quadruple Chocolate Chunk Cookies, 130
Quick breads, *see also* Muffins
    Chocolate Cherry Loaf, 156
    Cinnamon Pecan Cupcakes (v), 161

R

Raisins
Apple Raisin Sauce, 181
Oatmeal Cinnamon Raisin
Cookies, 124
Raspberries
Berry Pie, 137
Chocolate Raspberry
Brownies, 132
Raspberry Sauce, 180
Raspberry Vinaigrette, 50
Red Hot Chili, 78
Red peppers, *see* Peppers, Bell;
Chile Peppers
Ribs
Hot and Spicy BBQ Rub, 83
Roasted Chicken Garlic Salad
Sandwiches, 42
Roasted Corn and Pepper Salsa, 32
Roasted Pecan Pumpkin Soup, 59
Roasted Red Pepper Guacamole
Dip, 30
Roasted Red Pepper Velvet
Sauce, 178
Roasted Tomato Parmesan Soup,
56
Roasted Vegetables, 97
Rolls, *see also* Breads
Cheddar Cheese Rolls, 110
Crusty French Rolls, 114
Potato Rolls, 108
Whole Wheat Rolls, 112
Romano cheese, about, 11
Potato Cheese Soufflé, 90
Vegetable Almond Medley **(v)**,
94
Tomato Basil Tart, 93
Rosemary
Fresh Dill Mayonnaise **(v)**, 37
Fresh Tarragon Dill Bread **(v)**,
104
Rubs
Hot and Spicy BBQ Rub, 83
Jamaican Seafood Rub, 82

S

Salad dressings
Avocado Tamarind Cashew
Dressing, 49
Blue Cheese Peppercorn
Dressing, 48
Chipotle Mayonnaise, 38
Creamy French Salad
Dressing, 46
Fresh Dill Mayonnaise, 37
Homemade Ketchup **(v)**, 176
Raspberry Vinaigrette, 50
Thousand Island Dressing, 47
Traditional Mayonnaise, 36
Salads
Blue Cheese Peanut Coleslaw,
41
Cold Shrimp Salad, 65
Egg Salad Spread, 43
Pepper Pasta Salad, 44
Roasted Chicken Garlic Salad
Sandwiches, 42
Seafood Pâté, 66
Salami
Egg Salad Spread, 43
Pepper Pasta Salad **(v)**, 44
Stuffed Chicken Breasts, 75
Salmon
Macadamia-Crusted Salmon,
64
Salmon Herb Mousse on
Stone-Ground Crackers, 16
Salsa
Peach Mango Salsa, 33
Roasted Corn and Pepper
Salsa, 32
Tomatillo Onion Avocado
Salsa, 31
Traditional Salsa, 34
Sauces
Apple Raisin Sauce, 181
Avocado Tamarind Cashew
Dressing **(v)**, 49
Fresh Herb Tomato Dipping
Sauce, 175
Garden Fresh Pesto Sauce, 177
Raspberry Sauce, 180
Roasted Red Pepper Velvet
Sauce, 178
Smoked Chili Sauce, 174
Tomato Sauce, 179
Sausage
Fast and Easy Meat Loaf, 77
Grande Beef Nachos, 22
Savory Buttery Tart Pastry **(v)**,
139
Tomato Basil Tart, 93
Savory Chicken Cheese Balls, 27
Scallops
Cold Shrimp Salad **(v)**, 65
Drunken Fresh Herb
Marinade, 84
Jamaican Seafood Rub, 82
Seafood Pâté **(v)**, 66
Three Herb-Crusted Scallops,
68
Scones
Almond Poppy Seed Scones,
168
Chocolate Chip Scones, 169
Fresh Savory Herb Scones,
166
Peach Scones, 167
Seafood
Cold Shrimp Salad, 65
Drunken Fresh Herb
Marinade, 84
Jamaican Seafood Rub, 82
Seafood Pâté, 66
Shrimp Pâté with Leeks, 17
Three Herb-Crusted Scallops,
68
Shrimp
Cold Shrimp Salad, 65
Jamaican Seafood Rub, 82
Seafood Pâté, 66
Shrimp Pâté with Leeks, 17
Smoked Chili Sauce, 174
Mini Chicken Puffs, 24
Thousand Island Dressing, 47
Soups
Caramelized Onion and
Mushroom Soup, 52
Chanterelle Oyster Bisque
Soup, 55
Hearty Cauliflower and
Asparagus Soup, 60
Navy Bean Soup, 58
New England Clam Chowder,
54
Potato Leek Cheese Soup, 53
Roasted Pecan Pumpkin
Soup, 59
Roasted Tomato Parmesan
Soup, 56
Roasted Vegetables **(v)**, 97
Sour cream
Blue Cheese Peppercorn
Dressing, 48

Caramelized Onion and
Mushroom Soup, 52
Savory Chicken Cheese Balls,
27
Spiced Pastry, 135
Spices, about, 13
Spinach
Chicken Rockefeller, 76
Portobello Mushroom
Lasagna, 88
Seafood Pâté, 66
Strawberries
Berry Pie, 137
Strawberry Almond Cookies,
122
Stuffed Chicken Breasts, 75
Sugar and Spice Cookies, 129
Sun-Dried Tomato Pesto Bread,
106
Sunflower seeds
Honey Whole Wheat
Sunflower Bread, 102
Jamaican Seafood Rub, 82
Sweet peppers, *see* Peppers, bell
Swiss cheese, about, 11
Cheddar Cheese Rolls (v), 110
Mushroom-Stuffed Pork
Chops, 79

T
Tarragon
Drunken Fresh Herb
Marinade, 84
Fresh Tarragon Dill Bread, 104
Tarragon Dill Butter, 39
Tarts, *see* Pies and tarts
Thai Beef Skewers in Peanut
Sauce, 19
The Perfect Fudgey Brownie, 131
Thousand Island Dressing, 47
Three Herb-Crusted Scallops,
68
Three-Nut Cheesecake, 152
Thyme
Fresh Tarragon Dill Bread (v),
104
Tarragon Dill Butter (v), 39
Tomatillo Onion Avocado Salsa,
31
Tomatoes
Cold Shrimp Salad, 65
Eggplant Parmesan, 96

Fresh Herb Tomato Dipping
Sauce, 175
Homemade Ketchup, 176
Mini Meatballs with Garlic
Tomato Sauce, 20
New England Clam Chowder
(v), 54
Red Hot Chili, 78
Roasted Chicken Garlic Salad
Sandwiches, 42
Roasted Corn and Pepper
Salsa, 32
Roasted Red Pepper
Guacamole Dip (v), 30
Roasted Tomato Parmesan
Soup, 56
Tomato Basil Tart, 93
Tomato Sauce, 179
Traditional Salsa, 34
Traditional Mayonnaise, 36
Blue Cheese Peanut Coleslaw,
41
Blue Cheese Peppercorn
Dressing, 48
Cold Shrimp Salad, 65
Crispy Chicken Cakes with
Fresh Dill Mayonnaise, 25
Deviled Eggs with Caviar,
23
Egg Salad Spread, 43
Roasted Red Pepper Velvet
Sauce, 178
The Perfect Fudgey Brownie,
131
Thousand Island Dressing, 47
Tomato Basil Tart, 93
Traditional Salsa, 34
Turkey
Pepper Pasta Salad (v), 44
Turkey, ground
Fast and Easy Meat Loaf (v),
77
Turkey Meatballs, 74
Tuscan Pork Chops, 80
24 Carrot Cake, 158

V
Vanilla, about, 14
Vanilla Sugar, 119
Vegetables
Blue Cheese Peanut Coleslaw,
41

Crab Feta Mushrooms, 18
Eggplant Parmesan, 96
Grilled Portobello Mushrooms
with Balsamic Vinegar, 87
Pecan Yams, 98
Portobello Mushroom
Lasagna, 88
Potato Cheese Soufflé, 90
Potatoes au Gratin, 92
processing, 13
Pumpkin Purée, 86
Roasted Corn and Pepper
Salsa, 32
Roasted Red Pepper
Guacamole Dip, 30
Roasted Vegetables, 97
slicing and shredding, 13
Tomatillo Onion Avocado
Salsa, 31
Tomato Basil Tart, 93
Traditional Salsa, 34
Vegetable Almond Medley, 94
Vinaigrette, *see* Salad dressings

W
Walnuts
Honey Apple Spice Muffins
(v), 163
Peach Scones (v), 167
Three-Nut Cheesecake, 152
Whole Wheat Rolls (v), 112
White Cake, 160
Whitefish
Macadamia-Crusted Salmon
(v), 64
Seafood Pâté, 66
Whole Wheat Rolls, 112
Wine
Baked Beef Burgundy, 81
California Wine and Cheese
Bread, 100
Hearty Cauliflower and
Asparagus Soup, 60

Y
Yams
Pecan Yams, 98
Roasted Vegetables, 97
Yeast, about, 13

More Great Books
from Robert Rose

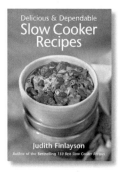

Appliance Cooking

- 125 Best Microwave Oven Recipes
  by Johanna Burkhard
- The Blender Bible
  by Andrew Chase and Nicole Young
- The Mixer Bible
  by Meredith Deeds and Carla Snyder
- The 150 Best Slow Cooker Recipes
  by Judith Finlayson
- Delicious & Dependable Slow Cooker Recipes
  by Judith Finlayson
- 125 Best Vegetarian Slow Cooker Recipes
  by Judith Finlayson
- 125 Best Rotisserie Oven Recipes
  by Judith Finlayson
- 125 Best Food Processor Recipes
  by George Geary
- The Best Family Slow Cooker Recipes
  by Donna-Marie Pye
- The Best Convection Oven Cookbook
  by Linda Stephen
- 125 Best Toaster Oven Recipes
  by Linda Stephen
- 250 Best American Bread Machine Baking Recipes
  by Donna Washburn and Heather Butt
- 250 Best Canadian Bread Machine Baking Recipes
  by Donna Washburn and Heather Butt

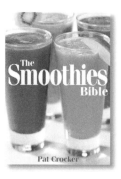

Baking

- 250 Best Cakes & Pies
  by Esther Brody
- 500 Best Cookies, Bars & Squares
  by Esther Brody
- 500 Best Muffin Recipes
  by Esther Brody
- 125 Best Cheesecake Recipes
  by George Geary
- 125 Best Chocolate Recipes
  by Julie Hasson
- 125 Best Chocolate Chip Recipes
  by Julie Hasson
- 125 Best Cupcake Recipes
  by Julie Hasson
- Complete Cake Mix Magic
  by Jill Snider

Healthy Cooking

- 125 Best Vegetarian Recipes
  by Byron Ayanoglu with contributions from Algis Kemezys
- America's Best Cookbook for Kids with Diabetes
  by Colleen Bartley
- Canada's Best Cookbook for Kids with Diabetes
  by Colleen Bartley
- The Juicing Bible
  by Pat Crocker and Susan Eagles
- The Smoothies Bible
  by Pat Crocker

- 125 Best Vegan Recipes
  by Maxine Effenson Chuck and Beth Gurney
- 500 Best Healthy Recipes
  Edited by Lynn Roblin, RD
- 125 Best Gluten-Free Recipes
  by Donna Washburn and Heather Butt
- The Best Gluten-Free Family Cookbook
  by Donna Washburn and Heather Butt
- America's Everyday Diabetes Cookbook
  Edited by Katherine E. Younker, MBA, RD
- Canada's Everyday Diabetes Choice Recipes
  Edited by Katherine E. Younker, MBA, RD
- Canada's Complete Diabetes Cookbook
  Edited by Katherine E. Younker, MBA, RD
- The Best Diabetes Cookbook (U.S.)
  Edited by Katherine E. Younker, MBA, RD
- The Best Low-Carb Cookbook
  from Robert Rose

Recent Bestsellers

- 125 Best Soup Recipes
  by Marylin Crowley and Joan Mackie
- The Convenience Cook
  by Judith Finlayson
- 125 Best Ice Cream Recipes
  by Marilyn Linton and Tanya Linton

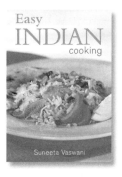

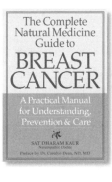

- Easy Indian Cooking
  by Suneeta Vaswani
- Simply Thai Cooking
  by Wandee Young and Byron Ayanoglu

Health

- The Complete Natural Medicine Guide to the 50 Most Common Medicinal Herbs
  by Dr. Heather Boon, B.Sc.Phm., Ph.D., and Michael Smith, B.Pharm, M.R.Pharm.S., ND
- The Complete Kid's Allergy and Asthma Guide
  Edited by Dr. Milton Gold
- The Complete Natural Medicine Guide to Breast Cancer
  by Sat Dharam Kaur, ND
- The Complete Doctor's Stress Solution
  by Penny Kendall-Reed, MSc, ND, and Dr. Stephen Reed, MD, FRCSC
- The Complete Doctor's Healthy Back Bible
  by Dr. Stephen Reed, MD, and Penny Kendall-Reed, MSc, ND, with Dr. Michael Ford, MD, FRCSC, and Dr. Charles Gregory, MD, ChB, FRCP(C)
- Everyday Risks in Pregnancy & Breastfeeding
  by Dr. Gideon Koren, MD, FRCP(C), ND
- Help for Eating Disorders
  by Dr. Debra Katzman, MD, FRCP(C), and Dr. Leora Pinhas, MD

Wherever books are sold